WE AR

These true supernatural stories are verified by many witnesses, who have experienced the miraculous intervention of God in this present age.

In my many years of teaching and administration at Oral Roberts University, I have had the opportunity to become personally acquainted with people who really know God and talk to Him and hear His voice. I can say without a doubt that Alan Youngblood knows God and talks to Him and hears directly from Him. My husband, Ben Martin, has been closely involved with Alan in many of the situations he describes in this book and has told him for years he must share this with the world. He verifies that every word is true and happened just the way Alan has described.

Voice of Many Waters will inspire you to desire to hear God and know what He wants you to do now and in the future. You will have a new glimpse of heaven and the end days and know your role in the great unfolding of God's plans and purposes for us, His most loved children.

—**Dr. Cherie Dawson Martin**
Former Associate Vice President for Academic Affairs
Oral Roberts University

This book is a labor of love from Pastor Alan and Barbara to everyone who will read it. I believe it will open blind eyes to the truth of Who God is and how much He wants to be included in all we do. As you turn the pages and see God work through the lives of those represented here, you can't help but experience His power and love—and an undeniable knowledge that

He wants to do the same for you. I am thankful to Pastor Alan for his obedience to share God's voice in his life and give others the opportunity to know the voice of God.

—**Shanna Gregor,** Author, Editor

You are invited into our lives. Come and stay awhile with us. Everything you will ever need will be provided through these intriguing, life-changing stories that we will share with you. As we sit, chatting, sipping hot coffee, don't be surprised if we are interrupted by our frequent celestial visitors, who are always welcome. You will find it impossible not to notice our always present, ever-abiding house guest, who lingers close by with a heavenly soft tissue in His nail-scarred hands, ready to wipe away every tear that will surely fall.

The door is unlocked; the lamp is on. We are sitting by a warm fire, just waiting for you.

Welcome to our world.

—**Barbara Youngblood**

Betrayed and devastated, I was left alone, trembling, overlooking the abyss of a life without a husband and raising four children on my own. When all my dreams had vanished, with nothing but a small glimmer of hope, I took my stand upon the Word of God, which changed my life forever.

If this book finds you in the midst of sorrow, trapped hopelessly in despair, you will be inspired and challenged when you read the stories of people whose lives were transformed from tragedy to triumph.

—**Joan Vandergriff**, N.D.

I hated lunch time at school. The possibility of me choking and being unable to breathe hung over me like a death sentence. Frightened and embarrassed, hoping my friends did not notice, I would duck my head near the bottom of the table, pushing food down my throat with my fingers. More than this, my greatest fear was our house catching on fire, and being unable to get out of bed, I would die there. My nightly prayer became more about my house not catching on fire than for my healing.

Then God sent His Word and healed me of the dreadful, crippling disease of muscular dystrophy! Come, take my hand and walk with me through the pages of this book of miracles. Before we finish, you too may experience the miraculous as I have.

—Tamara Youngblood Wright

I stood alone in my kitchen, crying uncontrollably, allowing my tears to splash like falling rain upon the pages of this precious book, recalling the saddest memories of my life, but yet savoring the greatest triumph of my mother's as Alzheimer's bowed its knee.

In this book you will find hope for those who are suffering from this debilitating disease.

—Sue Thompson, R.N.

Every life is a journey! Only God knows the distance we will travel and the paths we will take. In your travels through this book, you will enter the gates of heaven and hear the voices of millions singing. Then you will return inspired and encouraged, able to climb every mountain and fearing not the lowest valley.

You will come to know personally the One Who will never leave you; your fellow traveler, friend, and guide.

—Tricia Youngblood/Jenson OTR

Warning! *Voice of Many Waters* is an open book of fascinating warfare, inspirationally told by a true living warrior. When you finish the reading, you will be supernaturally trained, able to take on all manner of sickness, including Lucifer and his fallen legions. These gripping stories have been written for such a time as this.

Come, make your reservations, and ride with us as we follow the mightiest Warrior of all into history and humanity's final victorious battle.

—**David Gregg,** fellow warrior

How can I not believe in angels and the divine intervention of a supernatural God who saved me from certain death? Early one morning, I stepped down into a flooded room equipped with electrical floor plugs that were gurgling, sending smoke up to the surface. I stood there perplexed, yet without fear, knowing that my guardian angels were there to protect and keep me from all harm.

—**Taleesa Youngblood Wright**

Alan has been a mentor, friend, pastor and strong spiritual influence in my life for the past twenty-eight years. I was there to witness many of the events you will read about in this book. The most notable to which I can attest is the story of his daughter, Tamara, who was stricken with muscular dystrophy at fifteen years of age.

I personally witnessed the healing transformation of a crippled teenage girl into a complete, healthy, vibrant, whole, mature woman of God that she is today. I know this to be true because today . . . I am her husband.

—**Greg Wright**

I sat by the fire in a comfortable chair on a chilly night and listened to my friend retell the stories of the unwavering faithfulness of the one true God. He told of his personal transformation in a moment when time stood still. I felt the triumph of the widow's faith when Alan saw her husband sitting before the throne of God in his distinctive handmade suit.

These inspirational stories glorify God and inspire faith. They will encourage you; they encouraged me!

—**Sam Soleyn**

VOICE OF MANY WATERS

VOICE OF MANY WATERS

IRREFUTABLE EVIDENCE OF LIFE AFTER DEATH

ALAN YOUNGBLOOD

WinePressPublishing
Your Book, Defined.

WinePress Publishing (PO Box 428, Enumclaw, WA 98022) functions only as book publisher. As such, the ultimate design, content, editorial accuracy, and views expressed or implied in this work are those of the author.

ISBN 13: 978-1-60615-047-4
ISBN 10: 1-60615-047-2
Library of Congress Catalog Card Number: 2010922911

To Barbara, my eternal love, without you none of this would have ever been!

Second, not last, and certainly not least—my sainted mother, my mentor and friend.

These stories were written for our daughters and their husbands, Mark, Greg, and Jay,

Our daughters—Taleesa—our first, in the image of her mother, Charlotte—our second, waiting at the Gates of Pearl, Tamara—our third, so much like me, yet so much better, Tricia—our fourth, forever the baby.

Our grandchildren—London, Chandon, Isaac, Caydon, Isaiah, Justice, Moriah, and Journey.

And I heard as it were the voice of a great multitude, and as the voice of many waters, and as the voice of mighty thundering, saying, Alleluia: for the Lord God omnipotent reigns.

—Revelation 19:6 KJV

Contents

ACKNOWLEDGMENTS

God gave me a gift, a picture puzzle, with pieces scattered in a lidless box. They consisted of problems too difficult for me to solve. At times I found myself in situations no human could resolve. Then He added to them supernatural visions, personal visitations, and heavenly voices that would astonish and confound me, causing temporary mental paralysis and at times leaving me numb.

Then the most challenging instruction ever came when He spoke with an audible voice and said, "Write the book!"

With my limited experience, a book such as this could not have been written without the contributions of many. My heartfelt thanks go to all those who have in various ways contributed to making this book a reality.

First and foremost, my wife, who pieced together hundreds of fragments and made them into readable sentences, compiling and reliving episode after episode. Thank you for helping me through the frustrating times and cleaning up the hundreds of wadded balls of yellow notebook paper. I couldn't have done this without you!

Words cannot express the depths of my gratitude and devotion to Barbara, my wife, Taleesa, Tamara, and Tricia, our daughters, Greg Wright, Mark Wright, and Jay Jenson, our sons-in-law, grandchildren London, Chandon, Isaac, Caydon, Isaiah, Justice, Moriah, and Journey, my sister, Sue, and her husband, Bernie Thompson. It would have been impossible to have chosen any greater people than you to walk with me on this journey as my family. To those who wait at the gates, you too were an important part of this book—Mom, Dad, Dennis, baby Charlotte, and Barbara's dad, Rev. Junior Vandergriff. My love and adoration go to all of you!

I owe a huge debt of gratitude to my editor, Shanna Gregor, who brought energy, creativity, and skill to the writing and the quality of these stories, molding them into their final form. The book you now hold in your hand is due largely to her gifts and unselfish sacrifices.

Special thanks to Ben Martin, who through the years, pressed me to write this book. His wife, Cherie, listened with a knowledgeable ear, giving graceful praise that was wanted but unmerited.

A host of family and friends listened to me relate the stories again and again. Their excitement brought renewed courage for me to continue. Though you are unnamed, you are appreciated, loved, and always will be remembered.

It took all of you and your contributions, but more than these, the faithfulness of the Holy Spirit to complete the puzzle that reveals clearly the objective—to see and hear the heart of the Living God!

INTRODUCTION

God's greatest desire for you is that you become familiar with His voice and know Him personally!

My view of God was tainted—not by my sainted mother, but by the rigid influence of the church I grew up in. Its "book of rules" was impossible to follow. I was certain there wasn't anyone who could obey them, not even those who had written them.

It seemed to me the God of heaven was not a friendly God. Understanding that everything about Him was holy rendered Him unapproachable in my mind. I was fully convinced the mighty God was out to get us, to catch us and throw us into the lake of fire.

With all the rules and God's unattainable holy attributes, heaven seemed unreachable to me. In my mind, it was a fact that only a relatively small number of humans was qualified to enter into His awesome presence. And I was certain I was *not* one of these.

This is what I believed until that fateful, chilly Friday evening in December when an angel entered my pickup truck unannounced, coming without my solicitation. The abruptness of his appearing was stunning and surprised me. He claimed without reluctance as he entered my space to deliver a message from the Living God. In a booming, audible voice he said, "Ask God to reveal Himself unto you!"

As you turn the pages of this book you will see that this angel was a force to be reckoned with, and I found him difficult to discount. The voice—so compelling—his superior strength creating such intensity that I knew he could not be a natural being. Quickly, my resistance was broken. I gave in reluctantly, yet weakly to the demands of my uninvited guest.

With my mouth, I obeyed the compelling voice, but in my mind, it was impossible to comprehend that the Creator, maker of all things, wanted to reveal Himself to me. *Was it possible, could it be true, and how would He do it?* This became the greatest mystery revealed to me—just a mortal man!

As you read these provoking stories, look inside the heart and mind of this incredible Living God and explore and experience His great love and care that He longs to provide to you. Each of these true experiences will carry you back into the past, bring you into the present, and propel you into the future.

This book is not for the faint of heart. Prepare yourself for true adventures of a lifetime, not natural as man would tell them, but supernatural as only God could unveil them. Unleash your spiritual imagination and gasp for your breath along with me, as one moment you and I are here on the earth, and then we are carried through the gates of pearl to the throne of God. Through my eyes you will see the awe-inspiring walls of jasper and read what is written upon its green chalcedony walls, as we glide together like snow-white swans above the river of life that flows, meandering, beneath and beside the suspended streets of transparent gold.

You and I can join the mass multitudes. They cannot be numbered as they cry out with boisterous praise, singing Alleluia. The crescendo of their sounds comes together with the thundering of mighty waterfalls crashing down from the throne of God!

Though I could not see this enormous multitude of worshippers, their combined voices sounded like the voice of many waters and the voice of mighty thundering, saying, "Alleluia: for the Lord God omnipotent reigns" (Rev. 19:6 kjv).

As your trembling fingers turn the pages, you will plunge from the pinnacle of the splendor of heaven into the abyss. Through a broken-down door, you will witness the cold and bloody murder of my beloved brother and experience the power of forgiveness. In the midst of despair, a call will come from the throne of God.

Becoming familiar with His voice and dependent upon His presence, in the time it takes to snap my fingers, He seemed to disappear. Then the silence became deafening!

You will learn the power hidden in His words: powerful enough to set every captive free. You will learn how the skill of His surgical knife penetrated into the marrow of the bone or mended a complex nervous system as it did for my fifteen-year-old daughter, who was ravaged by a killer named muscular dystrophy, and released one person's memory from Alzheimer's so she could recognize her loved ones once again.

Experience the voice of God through these incredible miracles He has shared with me in the lives of people I love and know personally. Join me on the journey and see people set free from depression, fear, and loneliness, proving that this incredible God wants to reveal Himself to all humanity. You will meet face to face the spirit of fear and death, and you will not only survive, but also will be able to conquer every foe.

At last, we will mount upon the back of a great white stallion following the One Whose robe is stained with blood and on His head are many crowns. We will ride like the wind down from the heavens as mighty warriors to fight our last and final battle—the battle of Armageddon!

Are you ready? Let's get started!

CHAPTER 1

THE ENCOUNTER

"Thank God it's Friday!" It was the second week of December of 1980. All the elements surrounding my life seemed to be in control, creating a perfect world—as if I had designed it myself. The construction company I owned was producing a large gross income. My wife and I, with our three daughters, were a model family in our church and community. We lived in a new English Manor home that we had designed, built, and beautifully decorated. The church we attended and had helped establish from its beginning was enjoying a wonderful new facility. Oh, yes, my commercial softball team was one of the finest in the Dallas-Fort Worth area. I was driving along thinking, *How much better could life be?*

With all these thoughts running through my head, my heart swelled with pride as I drove along a back road, over the dam of a gorgeous lake between my home and business. I had no warning that my perfect world I had created was only moments away from invasion by an unseen and uninvited visitor.

Out of nowhere, something or someone entered my pickup truck, filling the cab with a suffocating presence. It felt as if every square inch of oxygen was consumed by a force I could not see—but I could *feel* it.

I struggled with reason—trying to comprehend what was happening! *Who had entered into my truck? Was it God or an angel?* Whoever or whatever it was had not been invited into my space. The interruption of my life was not anticipated nor was it wanted. Shaken, I drove further down the road, stunned by what was happening. Then I heard a voice.

The voice spoke to me audibly with words so profound I found it nearly impossible to believe what I was hearing—but it was real. I heard the words, "Ask God to reveal Himself unto you." Startled and completely bewildered, I wondered, *What in the world is this?* I am a person who has always refrained from anything that could alter my thinking. It was always important to me to be in control of my thoughts and the decisions I make.

But something invaded my vehicle, took over the air space I was breathing, and continued to speak to me with an audible voice. Someone I could not see said, "Ask God to reveal Himself unto you."

Usually, fear does not seize me; but this was becoming scary. Carefully, I pulled to the side of the road, trying to gather my thoughts. Sitting there, I pondered . . . *Am I going crazy? What is this?* Again the voice spoke, more demanding and forceful, commanding me, "Ask God to reveal Himself unto you."

My spirit knew this was real, but my mind was having a hard time comprehending it. I believed events like this happened in the Bible, as with Paul on the road to Damascus when he heard the voice of God. But I didn't understand how this could possibly happen to me. *What was this?*

So many times, I stood and gazed into the night sky, on more than one occasion wondering—*Is it possible you exist? How could you look down here on earth and see all the people? How could you know them, their personal thoughts, and the struggles they encounter? Is that even possible?* Traveling by airplane, I've questioned how in the world could God look down on the earth and see all the people He claimed He could see and know. *Was this true? It seemed beyond realism.*

Sitting there on the side of the road, my curiosity reached an all-time high. I had never encountered anything like this in my life nor known anyone who had. If someone had told me about an experience similar to this, I wouldn't have believed him!

Why would God, an angel, or some kind of presence, come into my vehicle and invade my space? Why would God, Who made the heavens and everything that exists, need me—a mere man—to ask Him anything? Why would God, Who lives somewhere way up in the heavens—encounter me? What could it mean—"Reveal Himself unto you" anyway?

My mother taught me to believe God existed. I knew of Him but not on a personal level—not as a God Who would come down to earth and talk with me. I didn't realize He wanted me to know Him. I thought I had a good understanding of Him. He was a great big God in the sky—one with His eye watching, attempting to catch me. He knew every mistake I had ever made, writing them down in some kind of book of sins in heaven. I believed they were gathered for the purpose of knowing all the sins I had committed, enabling Him to one day judge me. This was the kind of God I believed Him to be.

Shaken, I carefully maneuvered back onto the road and continued over the dam of the lake. The voice came again. This time it was so compelling, strong, and forceful, saying again, "Ask God to reveal Himself unto you." For a moment I gasped—crushed by the pressure of this uninvited being I could not see but whose voice I could hear.

Proceeding over the dam, I gazed into the heavens and whispered, "God, if You really are there . . . if You are the One they spoke about in Genesis 1, saying You created the heavens and earth and everything that exists . . . if You really did, then reveal Yourself unto me."

Immediately, expectancy was birthed within me. With excitement I proclaimed, "Wow! This is going to be good!" I was certain He could see me, but I couldn't see Him. Then the voice spoke again, softly and not as forceful, "Name a date; name a time."

No, no, no! This one thing I know, you don't put a time clock on God. There is no one who has the authority to control Him; you don't dictate anything to the Almighty. With resounding reluctance to put God on the clock, in my mind's eye, I saw Him—the Maker of all things, the Supreme Being Who alone does the dictating.

Once again the voice spoke in the same gentle way, "Name a date; name a time." Hesitantly, I stammered, "God, if You really are, if You do exist, if You made man as the Bible said, reveal Yourself unto me before the first of the year." Remember, this was mid-December 1980.

In the twinkling of an eye, his presence was gone, and the pressure was off. He disappeared as quickly as he came. Left alone with my meditations, I thought, *I can't tell anyone about this. They might think I'm going crazy. Besides, I may be. Who am I to think God, the Creator, would talk to me or send an angel with a request, revealing God's desire for me to become familiar with His voice so that I would know Him personally?*

In the vastness of my imaginations, I never dreamed this could be a reality in my life! Maybe it was like this in the days of Abraham or the apostle Paul—but for me, this has to be as wild as it gets! As I continued to drive over the lake road, I couldn't refrain from looking toward the heavens past the setting sun, into the cloudy, spacey areas of the sky, thinking, *Am I going to see God? Is there going to be a big sign in the sky, "I'm God?"* I looked for Him in the only place I knew—in the heavens! After all, that's where He lives! I saw nothing, nothing at all, even though it remained the most amazing moment of my life.

In the midst of my busy schedule, the event subsided from my memory. The holidays were upon us with many obligations of the season. We had reservations for a private Christmas dinner for our employees at a restaurant in Dallas; gifts to buy, the tree to trim, and all the things you do at Christmas. So much was happening as we moved toward the end of the year. We were busy and the days passed so swiftly. I couldn't find it within myself to reveal my encounter to anyone. How could I tell them anyway?

How do you bring up the conversation? Uh, God visited me in my vehicle the other day, or an angel showed up. Yeah, I heard him. He spoke with an audible voice. Yep, with a voice—a scary voice, a strong, compelling voice—an angelic voice I never expected to hear!

Never knowing anyone in a situation quite like this, I determined not to allow anyone to think I was losing my mind or getting overly religious. Conveniently, I let it slip from my mind.

It was the season for Christmas celebrations, family gatherings, church functions, parties, and shopping. As the days slipped away, I totally forgot about the date I had set. It never crossed my mind, seeming like it wasn't real; certainly nothing had happened.

The only troublesome time during the holiday season was my brother, Dennis, who lived in Oklahoma City and whom I had not seen in a number of months, came to see me. His world had turned upside down. Charlsie his wife, recently filed for divorce, separating him from His eight children. Everything concerning his life was in shambles.

Rarely had two brothers shared life as closely as we had. He was my *big* brother, but I was my brother's keeper. We sat and talked—he told me his troubles and concerns for his future, telling me he had a premonition he was going to die. This really frightened me.

I looked at him with tear-filled eyes, "Brother, would you ever take your own life?"

With anguish he shared with me the terrifying secret. "Two weeks ago, I prepared a will, leaving you as the executor. I left it in the file box beside the kitchen table, along with my life insurance policies and personal instructions to you. You will find a loaded pistol lying close by."

I gasped as he continued, "Three days ago, before I decided to come visit you, I placed the pistol to my head and tried to pull the trigger. With my eyes closed tightly, I saw Mother's face, with tears streaming from her eyes, her mouth quivering, as she prayed to God, asking Him to spare my life. Slowly, I released my finger from the trigger and carefully laid it aside. That's when I realized I could never take my own life!"

Relieved, yet not knowing what the future held for my brother, we embraced and held each other, as long as it was possible. Sadly, the next morning he returned home.

The following days went by swiftly, and it was December 31 before I even realized it. All the days had been full, but not all fun. A winter ice storm came to visit and lingered through the thirty-first. The roads were icy, with people slipping and sliding everywhere. On this closing day of the year, the last thing I wanted to do was exactly what we had always done—go to church. We celebrated the going out of the old year and the coming in of the new at our church. It was called the watch-night service.

I told my wife, "There's ice covering the roads and bridges and no one will be there! What's the wisdom of driving all the way across town on this ice? We could end up in a ditch somewhere."

Not buying my excuses, with disdain she said, "You drive further to work, and besides, we have a four-wheel-drive vehicle. We are going to church like we always do on the last night of the year." Not having any more reasonable excuses, disgruntled, I dressed and drove the family across town to fulfill our duty on New Year's Eve.

We arrived around 8:00 P.M. and I knew we would stay until midnight. It was drudgery for me: four hours of singing, testimonies, and praise reports—good and bad—of the past year. It was tradition . . . going on and on since I was a small child. It had been the same 'ole, same 'ole for thirty-eight years.

My mind was somewhere else—anywhere else . . . my softball team, our upcoming ski trip. Suddenly, a voice whispered. Possibly, this had happened to me many times over the years, but I sensed something different. In my mind, a thought entered in the form of words, an inward voice saying, *It's not going to happen.*

I thought, *What was that? Who said it?* It wasn't the same voice I had previously heard in my truck, similar but different from the other voice. I whispered to myself inwardly, "What's not going to happen?"

Then the voice again spoke inwardly, "God's not going to reveal Himself to you as you have requested. Here we are; it's almost 11:30 P.M." The voice continued in my thoughts, "He is not going to do it. Time is running out!"

I reasoned, *It's not up to me, but up to Him,* trying to sort it out in my head. Confusion raged in my mind, trying to take me hostage. Then, for the first time, I realized this voice was not God's voice, not my voice, but the voice of my adversary, the devil.

My spirit came alive and in my mind, I fought him. "Devil, it doesn't matter whether God shows up in person and declares 'I'm God,' or reveals Himself in the written Word! It doesn't matter to me if He does or does not, I know in my heart I believe in Him."

Trying to make an excuse, with confidence I responded, "Devil, I know He is real!" I said it with great conviction in my heart and, suddenly, I felt much better. Evidently, my declaration of faith in God convinced him. He fled from me quicker than he had come.

At this moment, my confession of the reality of God seemed to be what He wanted all along—to acknowledge Him and say, "He's real; I believe in Him."

Midnight crept closer as the pastor called for everyone to come forward to the altar and stand around in family units for communion. *Wait a minute! This isn't the way we always do this. Usually, we kneel down, men on one side and women on the other. The elders pass the cups of grape juice and bread. Then we are given the opportunity pray privately and ask forgiveness for our sins.*

My tradition was being shaken because I knew I couldn't take communion without confessing my sins. I preferred the old tradition, praying privately and silently. Convincing myself that no one knew of my inward three sins anyway, I tried to adjust to this new situation. After all, I had everything down pat; I was fine. *I might have three pet sins, but these aren't anyone's business.*

Feeling very uncomfortable, I trudged to the front of the church with my wife and my three daughters. Standing there, while each of us took a small plastic cup, in my mind, I was upset at this preacher! *What is he trying to pull? He's fouling everything up! My family is here and I'm struggling about my three sins being found out.* Frustrated, I decided to confess my sins secretly.

Our pastor called an elderly gentleman to pray over the cup. *He could preach a sermon with his prayers*, I thought. Holding a little plastic cup in my hand, with my eyes closed, waiting for his long prayer to conclude, the strangest thing in the history of my life occurred.

Instantly, I was carried away as he prayed—translated into heaven. I stood there, stunned, with only one thought. *My Lord, what is this?*

CHAPTER 2

TRANSFORMATION

Faster than my mind could conceive, I left my earthly body and was carried into the heavens, to the outer edge of a massive wilderness. It seemed to me that the evening was nearly spent. The gathering darkness was consuming the last rays of light, leaving just enough to dimly see a great high wall slightly beyond the outstretched limbs of enormous cedar trees, towering far above the mighty fortress' boundary. I could identify some of the trees, but I had never seen any that compared with these magnificent living monarchs.

But more bewildering than the massive size of these trees in the forest, was—*What am I doing here?* Frightened and stunned by this sudden change of location and standing in this unfamiliar setting, it happened!

I could not see Him, but I could hear His voice—the sound of many waters, rushing forward as He came near. His presence filled the atmosphere surrounding me. I stood there feeling guilty and unworthy, flooded with emotions I had never experienced before, and without words to express my feelings.

A transparent scroll unrolled out of my chest. On the scroll were words, spelling out my sins. Sure enough, there were three of them. But surprisingly, they were not the three I had privately confessed on many occasions. The names of each sin—ones I had never considered to be sin—were written there. The first one was pride.

Pride? Oh, God, You mean pride is wrong? I had so much pride in my life I was proud of my pride. I never knew there was any thing wrong with being proud of all your accomplishments. I was pleased with how I dressed, where I lived, and what I had done. But there it was—ugly PRIDE.

A scripture came to me. "These six things the Lord hates, yes, seven are an abomination to Him: A proud look, a lying tongue, hands that shed innocent blood, a heart that devises wicked plans, feet that are swift in running to evil, a false witness who speaks lies, and one who sows discord among brethren" (Prov. 6:16–19 NKJV).

There are seven things God hates, and number one is pride. I looked at the scroll and was astonished at what was inside me. Number two read, JUDGING. Oh, I had successfully removed God and placed myself upon the throne to judge everybody. I could judge someone by his or her appearance, by the clothes people wear, or what they do. The ones I judged were always found guilty.

Again the scripture came to me, "Who are you to judge another's servant? To his own master he stands or falls. Indeed, he will be made to stand, for God is able to make him stand" (Rom. 14:4 NKJV).

The third thing I saw on the scroll of my three sins was the word MURDERER. I felt frantic, *Oh, God! Who have I murdered? Who is it I have killed?* The scripture came to me,

"If anyone says, 'I love God,' yet hates his brother, he is a liar. For anyone who does not love his brother whom he has seen, cannot love God, whom he has not seen" (1 John 4:20 NIV). "If you say you love God and hate your brother, you are the same as a murderer" (1 John 3:15 NIV).

I had never hated my brother, but I hated many other people; men and women of various races, different churches, and those I felt had done me wrong. The last thing on earth I wanted to do was forgive *them*. If I forgave them, it would be letting them off the hook. They needed to pay for what they'd done to me. My feelings ran deep. Even if a person looked similar to someone I resented, I hated him or her too. Standing before the throne with a scroll coming out of my chest, I realized I had murdered—maybe thousands, because of my hatred. For the first time in my life, I felt guilty and undone. I was deeply sorry for my sins. I had seen them as God sees them. They were much different from what I had perceived my sins to be.

This was really me! These sins were mine and were coming out of my chest. The scripture says, "What's on the inside of man—not what's on the outside—is what defiles a man" (Matt. 15:18). These were inside of me. I saw them and was repentant for my sins.

Regretting the pride I had carried all those years and the judging I had rendered cruelly to many people, I was sorry for all those I hated and had never forgiven. I felt an inward explosion of deep regret, remorse for sins I had committed, and I felt sorry for people I had done wrong.

All of a sudden, forgiveness came to me. I was not forgiven by anyone else, but by God Himself. He cleansed me and made me whole. Never had I experienced so much peace. It overcame me. I knew, standing there, my sins had been forgiven and I no longer harbored feelings of bitterness and hatred toward anyone. My sins were gone!

For the first time, I *knew* I was right with God. His peace overwhelmed me, as great joy sprang up in my heart. I marveled, *This is the* greatest *experience.* It was one I had never had before.

Then I was carried past the high wall through a pair of open gates. They were tall, enormous and made of pearl—one large incredible pearl, fashioned into a gate. As I entered the celestial city, a bright light illuminated it with the brilliance of the noonday sun.

Turning, I saw the great wall I had seen from the outside surrounding God's paradise; it appeared to be made of jasper, a precious stone, opaque in appearance. The Word of God was written in various languages on the walls in multi-colors of green and blackish green quartz with raised white letters.

I floated two or three feet above the ground. When I looked down, I saw the streets below me. Yes, they were gold! I could see through them! They were transparent—so amazing. The streets of the city were not laid on dirt, but suspended, enabling me to see through them.

Rivers of water flowed beneath and beside them. The streets were as a suspended bridge without visible supports. I could hear a waterfall in the distance, greater than Niagara Falls. An enormous waterfall cascaded from the throne of God.

Quickly, I was carried up close to a platform with three steps, large and tall. Looking to the right, I could see the platform disappear in the distance. To my left was a rounded corner. It was beautifully made of marble unlike any I'd ever seen (and I've seen a lot of marble in my profession as a builder). It was all one piece—a gigantic slab with many colors. It was pink, beige, and brown, with areas of white. It flowed seamlessly together without joints, just one large piece.

Sitting on the bottom step of this platform I saw a man. I recognized him because he was a friend of mine. I had known him for many years, being raised in the same church together. He had expressed friendship to me on many occasions. On various Sunday afternoons he asked me to go with him because he desired to teach me how to fly.

His invitation was never accepted because I had other interests. My preference was football on Sunday afternoons, not flying in a plane. As I looked at him, I remembered he'd made a missionary trip with two other men to Mexico to deliver clothing, food, and other items. Their trip landed him in heaven.

On their fateful flight they came into a large fog of clouds. The instruments they needed failed to function, causing them to fly into the side of a mountain. Instantly, the plane exploded. Their bodies were scattered throughout the forest and mountains in Mexico. Amazingly, one man survived, but it was not my friend, Jerry Hardgrave. He had burned until there was practically nothing left of his remains. His body, along with the pilot's, were brought back to the States in body bags.

Now here Jerry was, sitting on the bottom of this beautiful step. Surprisingly, he didn't have on a robe. I thought, *Where is your white robe we were taught we would have in heaven?* There were no wings, but the clothes he wore were more interesting than I could have ever imagined. He was wearing a double-knit blue and white tweed coat with blue double-knit pants. He had on a white shirt with a tie made from the same matching material as the coat. His shoes were penny loafers.

I looked at his clothes and remembered when, some ten years before, Jerry and I had come across each other at church on Easter Sunday morning. Everyone dresses up in their finest on Easter to look their best. On that Sunday morning, I wore a fine tailored suit made for me in England with a silk tie and hankie in my pocket, jewelry, and alligator shoes. *I was looking good!*

Jerry came to me and complimented me on all of my finery. I had on the best of everything! Remember the pride? Jerry was a good man. He was kind and gentle, wanting to be my friend. I returned the compliment concerning the suit he was wearing; it was a blue tweed coat with blue double-knit pants with a matching tie made from the same fabric. He was wearing penny loafer shoes.

Showing politeness, I expressed my interest in the clothes he was wearing. Never had I seen a suit and tie made from the same material before. Pleased, he inquired, "Alan, do you like it?"

Hiding my true feelings, I said, "Jerry, it is different from any suit I have ever seen."

Smiling with secret pride, he confided, "My mother-in-law made it for me as a gift for Easter."

"Really!" I was impressed. The seams were sewn together nicely.

"Jerry, tell her what an excellent seamstress she is."

I was never to see this unique suit again . . . until now!

But there he was *in heaven,* wearing the exact same suit he wore on that fateful resurrection morning. In amazement, I stood transfixed, puzzled, trying to grasp the magnitude of the moment. With my own eyes, I saw Jerry before me, more alive than ever before; not a shadow nor a semblance of himself, but with the glorious fullness of the essence, revealing with clarity the perfect reflection of life after death.

Not of my own doing, but with divine appointment, I was sealed with the burning branding iron of the Holy Spirit as a living witness to the futility of a burning fuselage of the exploding airplane that became an incinerator, devouring his body. It had failed!

For there in heaven, Jerry was made whole, becoming more perfect and handsome than the original. His countenance was angelically enhanced by the inward radiance that glowed outward, shining brilliantly from his face, displaying the image of the One Who had made him.

As I looked into the depths of his smiling brown eyes, they spoke to me, uncovering the hidden secret of restoration. His eyes had beheld the Lord God Almighty, causing him to be transformed by the power of the resurrected Christ, thus raising him up into the fullness of eternal life. A broad, peaceful smile spread endlessly across his face. From his innermost being, like rivers of cascading waters, joy flowed freely out of him. Suddenly, I knew if I tried to convince him to return with me, he would kindly decline.

As I jealously admired him, I could not help but wonder why in God's world was he wearing the hand-made suit his mother-in-law had made for him? Mesmerized, I stood amazed, but still concerned. *Why the absence of a white robe?*

To my surprise, he held a small communion cup in his left hand between his fingers, just like the one I was gripping more tightly than ever. With an air of complacence, he sat there comfortably filled with contentment but undoubtedly amused at the ever-changing expressions of curiosity running rampant across my face. Shaking my head, with my eyes filled with questions, I stood there wondering, *Was he sitting here purposely awaiting my arrival?*

Then he spoke, shocking me out of my wits! I was speechless! Instantly, I realized Jerry could see me; he acknowledged me, calling my name. With an all-knowing look, he smiled as he turned, tilting his head upward with his left hand held high, pointing with the empty communion cup.

"Alan, there's the throne," he said.

I was astonished and even more fascinated now, and apprehension grabbed me as never before. I stood there breathless! It was the scariest moment in my life. *Was I going to see God face to face?* Hesitantly, in awe, I lifted my eyes slowly, glancing at each step of the platform.

As my eyes reached the highest level, I saw the carved wooden legs of a huge chair that were wrapped with buckles of transparent gold.

From the right side, bellowing clouds of white smoke began to move across the platform. Frightened, I yelled, "The smoke is alive! It's alive!" It moved! It had life! It wasn't lying there dormant, but it moved, covering the platform and the legs of the chair. As I watched in amazement, the chair disappeared. The living smoke had completely covered it.

Mystified, I brought my eyes back down to Jerry and looked at the cup he held in his hand. It was empty. Jerry had taken of the cup before my arrival. Smiling, he said, "Alan, take of the cup."

The next thing I knew, I stood at the front of the church, alone. My family and everyone else had gone back to their seats. I looked down at the cup still in my hand and quickly drank of it. Not understanding what had happened, I was embarrassed.

Standing there at the front of the church as if I'd been in a trance, I turned to go back and sit down with my family. My wife asked me, "What were you doing? Did you go to sleep?"

"No," I replied, "I didn't go to sleep."

She was troubled because I had been standing there in the front—just standing there, all by myself. It was two minutes until midnight! The congregation began to sing "Looking for a City" as the clock began to tick down.

But there was a difference now. I had been inside heaven and experienced things I thought no man could possibly ever experience. I had traveled somewhere I had never been before. All of my sins were washed away! The sins I thought were in a big book weren't in a big book after all. They were inside of me and now they were gone.

The people I had hated, I hated no more. The ones I had never forgiven were all forgiven. Those I had separated myself from, I now wanted to see. The ones I had resented and the losers I had overlooked, I became sensitive to.

I had never cried a tear I can remember; tears were for women and sissies. This hard position I had carried all the days of my life began to flow out of me. For the first time, tears came to my eyes, coming and going for more than three days. I could not stop weeping. I was not the same person—not ever again.

As we drove home, my wife asked, "What has happened to you?"

Trying to conceal the tears, I confided, "I'm not sure I can explain to you at this time what I experienced just before midnight. But later on, when I'm able to understand, I will attempt to tell you everything."

Looking at me with loving eyes, she said, "You look different; you act different. Are you okay?"

Wiping tears from my eyes without answering, I knew I *was* different! All my life I had made things happen with my high-tempered fits of anger exploding out of me at any moment. My life was transformed as I stood in the presence of the Living God. I wondered if this was the answer to my obedience in asking God to reveal Himself to me.

I looked forward to the day I could explain what had taken place this night and share this incredible encounter with my wife, friends, and especially my brother Dennis!

> "When I consider your heavens, the work of your fingers, the moon and the stars, which you have set in place, what is man that you are mindful of him, the son of man that you care for him? You made him a little lower than the heavenly beings, and crowned him with glory and honor."
>
> —Psalm 8:3–5

CHAPTER 3

MY BROTHER'S KEEPER

I was running as fast as I could. I had ten minutes to make it across the street to the Dairy Queen and back to the fifth-grade building, which was off-limits to a third grader. In Texas, September days are hot. I ordered my chocolate-dipped cone with the dime my mother had given me the night before. My brother and I had already eaten the Twinkies from my sack lunch.

Whoops! I forgot the napkin. I won't need it anyway. I'll just run faster! This peanut butter sandwich and Fritos® I had for lunch will give me extra speed. I ran down the hallway to room number twelve. Behind the door was my big brother, Dennis—the toughest fighter in our school. Kids said he could whip three boys at one time. *And I'm going to be just like him,* I thought.

Maybe not as good looking, but it would be close. At last there was room number twelve. My heart was pumping. The hot asphalt stuck to my tennis shoes. Looking at the ice cream as chocolate ran down my hand and hiding it behind my back, I was shaking and scared! The rumor was that this teacher was a big, mean woman—known to pull hair. Calming myself, I thought, *I don't care! It will be worth it so my brother can have the first lick and then I can eat what's left.*

With my arm behind me and the ice cream running down my hand, I tapped on the door. And there she stood—the meanest woman I had ever seen. Gasping out the words, "It's an emergency for my brother, Dennis." Seeing the panic in my eyes, quickly she turned and yelled, "Dennis, come to the door!"

She left us alone in the hallway and he stood there looking at me, bewildered.

"What do you want?" he questioned. *Now I was going to make him happy,* I thought. From behind my back, I revealed the prized soggy cone. The ice cream was dripping from my hand. There was no more chocolate to be seen. It was lying in a puddle behind me.

Looking at my idol with my melted treat held high, I said to him, "Take the first lick."

His blue eyes stared at me. "I don't want it," he said. My heart climbed to my throat, choking me with tears of disappointment. He looked down at me with compassion.

"Okay!" he replied, and grabbing my wrist, he took the first lick. Instantly, I was off and running, eating his melted ice cream, soggy cone and all.

Torn blue jeans, skinned elbows, fat lips, and bloody noses; those were the badges of courage of a good brawler. I couldn't wait! It was early September and school had just started. I had made it to the fourth grade. Feeling bigger than I was, I picked a fight with a fifth-grader after school in front of the softball backstop. A large circle formed. The troublemaker was almost a foot taller than I was, and his arms were more than twice the size of mine. Everyone was yelling—"Fight, you chicken!"

Looking across the ball field, at last I saw my big brother coming to join me.

Our eyes met and my blood began to flow faster. Looking at my hated enemy as I moved toward him, I was more than ready—knowing my big brother was close by.

Quickly the years flew past us and suddenly we were teenagers. The two of us became so different. I was taller, but he was better looking. I quit fighting, but he never did. Alcohol, brass knuckles, switchblades, and chains became his armament. He frequented jail cells, at least until I could get him out. The bars and clubs were his biggest nighttime hangout, even after his marriage.

Eight children later, he was still fighting—alcohol fueled his anger. He had abandoned the church where we both were raised and left the God of his childhood. I continued on without him. Often my wife, Barbara, and I drove across town to take food and clothing to his family. We wanted to make certain the children had adequate clothes for school and food to eat.

Late one evening, I arrived at his house while he was still at work. Lying in the front yard was the motor out of his old car, leaving the family without transportation and forcing him to catch the bus to downtown Ft. Worth every day. I felt a knife plunging into my innermost being with questions of how he was going to feed and clothe ten people. It shredded my emotions, stabbing me to the depths of my heart.

I pondered, *What can I do to help my brother?* Arriving home just before dark, I decided to share with Barbara the plight of my brother and his family. Immediately after dinner, we slipped away to the privacy of our bedroom. Through the years of our marriage, she had learned to read me like an open book. The expressions on my face and the tone of my voice notified her that something was desperately wrong.

With my heart aching, I stammered, "Honey, you know of my love for my brother. I am experiencing great difficulty living with myself, knowing we have two automobiles and my brother has none."

Sensing my frustration, she gently interrupted, "What is it you want to do?"

Pausing, I said, "You know me better than anyone else."

"Why don't we give him one of our cars?" she offered lovingly.

The next day we put new tires on the car and filled it with gas. We took it over to their house and parked it in the driveway, endorsing the clear title to him, with a little note explaining it was our gift to him and his family.

Dennis wasn't a person who would ask for help, but when you did help him, he insisted on returning the favor. It was decided he would come over on weekends and build the girls a playhouse, just like a real house with windows, porch, and roof. This was his way of showing his gratitude and love for me. Looking back, this was the pleasure of having a brother— giving and sharing life with someone you loved.

I've looked at my life many times, remembering the story about Cain and Abel. When God asked Cain, "Do you know where your brother is?" Cain responded sarcastically, "Am I my brother's keeper?" (Gen. 4:9). I decided very early in my childhood that, because of my deep love and commitment to Dennis, I would be my brother's keeper!

The years swiftly went by. Dennis moved from Ft. Worth to Oklahoma City, being employed by the government. He worked on the eleventh floor of the Murray Building, which became famous when a terrorist bombed the building, killing innocent men, women, and children.

When he moved, my heart was perplexed. I wondered, *Who will take care of him now? Who will see about the children?* I knew I couldn't be there as often as I wanted to be for him. The only way I could find any peace was to fully believe God would be there for him. Jesus says, "I am a friend who sticks closer than a brother" (Prov. 18:24). This was the kind of friend I knew Dennis was going to need.

I comforted myself knowing God would be there for him at all times; knowing He would never leave him nor forsake him, but would be with him to the end. No matter how far my brother had traveled from God, He had never left him. God still loved and watched over him. The faithful God would prove Himself as this kind of friend.

Just fourteen days had passed since my life had changed on that fateful New Year's Eve night—when I stood before the throne of God in heaven. It was just like being born again. Peace and joy flooded my soul like a cleansing river, as my heart was emptied of hate and the anger that had poured out of my innermost being.

As I stood before the merciful God, all of my sins came out of me. Instead of judging and sending me to a devils' hell, God totally set me free—free from the many things I had done to myself. Some were of my own doing or from my enemy, who had tricked and used me. All of my sinful passions I once had were gone!

The people at church commented, saying I didn't even look like the same person. And I *wasn't* the person I had been before. I had found it impossible to change myself. Had I been able to, I would have accomplished it many years before.

On Wednesday night, we sang songs from the hymnbook and the pastor shared the gospel message. He gave us the opportunity to pray at the conclusion of the service. Going forward, I knelt at the altar and closed my eyes. Suddenly, a voice whispered in my ear, "Dennis is dying in Oklahoma City." I gulped! Instantly, I was dazed by this statement.

My thoughts exploded, *I'm here; he's there. I can't get to him! If I could, I would be there kneeling by his side.* Fear gripped my heart, and nausea overcame my stomach. My head was spinning! I would assure him God was there to save him.

Remembering my mother's voice when she was afraid, she would always "plead the blood of Jesus," over whomever she was concerned about. Inwardly, I screamed, "I plead the blood of Jesus over his eternal soul. Please, God, don't let him go to hell!"

Amazingly, the dizziness began to ease. Peace found an entrance into my aching heart, and with confidence I knew the faithful God would be there for my brother.

As we drove home after church, Barbara asked, "Honey, why are you so quiet?"

I shared with her the premonition from the voice I heard while I was praying at the end of the service.

Gravely concerned, she said, "When we get home you need to call Dennis and make sure he is okay."

Upon arrival at home, as we were changing our clothes and preparing for bed, the telephone rang. The answering machine picked up on the second ring, and the troubled voice on the other end spoke. "This is the Oklahoma City police."

In a rush, I grabbed the phone. Immediately, gripping the receiver with my clammy hand, I cried, "Is my brother dead?"

Silence . . . silence met me with a deafening voice on the other end of the telephone.

"How did you know?" he stuttered.

Pressing him with urgency, I asked, "What has happened?"

"Your brother was pronounced dead forty-five minutes ago, after he was shot." The officer's words hung in the air like dark bellowing clouds of smoke.

My first thoughts were, *He was killed in a bar or a fight.*

The officer stammered, "At 8:00 P.M. Dennis showed up at his house where he had once lived. The door being locked, he decided to *forcefully* enter to see his children. Charlsie, his wife, stood in the hallway with a loaded pistol. As he stepped toward her she pulled the trigger."

My mind was racing . . . *she shot him . . . she shot him and killed him in cold blood!*

The officer was still speaking. "She said he staggered toward her, put his arms around her, looking into her face with an angelic look. She saw with her own eyes, peace spread across his face, like she had never seen before."

One of his children called 9-1-1. When the emergency paramedics arrived, Dennis was still alive; he lingered for forty-five minutes. He was lying there, fighting for his life, incredibly at the precise time the merciful God spoke to me about him dying in Oklahoma City. From the splendor of heaven where I had ascended, I began to plunge, descending to the depths of the abyss. It was impossible to find sleep that night. Because of my brother's sudden death, I inherited the role I never wanted—of being the "big brother" for my sister. It became my lot to call and tell her the horrible news.

With a broken heart, my mind lost in a heavy fog, at midnight Barbara and I searched our way across the city to where my mother and father lived, calling them in advance of our arrival. Smothered with grief, with my heart pounding, I knocked on their door at 1:30 A.M. With only a dim porch light revealing the agony on my face, Dad, heavily troubled, answered the door, with Mom clinging to his side. As I reached for her, in terror she cried out, "Is it Dennis? Is it Dennis? What has happened to Dennis?"

I grabbed her into my arms and with our hearts shattered into a thousand pieces, we made our way into their living room. With me, it was impossible, but with the help of the Comforter, I was able to tell them the horrible story of what had happened hours before. Mom, grasping me with her long, thin fingers, looked into my tear-filled eyes and told me she had been awakened and also prayed for Dennis at the very time of his death.

I could not sleep; it was impossible. I walked through the daze of the heartbreak I was in. Death was the most devastating enemy I had ever encountered. It was the most formidable foe I had ever faced, more sudden and sickening than my mind could ever imagine, leaving my emotions in a state of semi-consciousness.

I heard voices of guilt that would not shut up: *If only I had been there I could have stopped this. You were there! Why, God, did you let this happen?* The accusing voices dogged me day and night without relenting.

In the midst of the voices, I heard one which sounded right, telling me it was my brotherly duty to kill the person who had taken his life. With joy, I would have given my life and laid it down sacrificially in Dennis' behalf. Pressured, I was faced with whether or not I should take the life of the one who took his.

This voice of reason continually whispered in my ear, "Your brother's blood cries out from the ground." I replayed the many times he had saved me—coming to my rescue as we were growing up. *Now, what can I do to bring justice to the memory of my brother? How can I know I did everything I could on behalf of him?*

Within twenty-four hours, I was on an airplane, flying to Oklahoma City. As I looked up into the heavens, I was comforted knowing God was there. I wondered how I was going to face the insurmountable mountain that faced me. I had purposed in my heart to claim my brother's body and bring him back home where he belonged. Barbara and I decided to give a grave plot we owned at Bluebonnet Hills Cemetery, where he could lie close to me someday.

As I pondered these things, little did I know, according to the laws of the State of Oklahoma, it would require documents concerning his death to be hand carried through legislation to release his body into my care, so I could bring him home to Texas.

Having been there before with Dennis, I returned to where he worked on the eleventh floor of the Murray Building. There I was greeted by his bereaved friends who worked with him. Lovingly, they told me what a wonderful person my brother was. With care, they brought me the boxes that held all of his personal belongings, sharing with me the many different memories they had experienced while working with him and what a friend he was.

They informed me that his closest friend was an African-American senator who worked in the capitol building. With encouragement to contact him, they placed in my hand a business card with his name and phone number. From Dennis' office I made the call and told him of my plight to get my brother's body released. With tearful good-byes, I made my way to the capitol building to the senator's office.

Upon entering his office, the next thing I knew we were hugging each other like brothers. The two of us had shared one common bond—we had loved the same person. I was there to get him; and he was there to help me.

Six and a half hours later, he had gathered all of the documents required to release my brother's body. This wonderful senator proved himself to be a great friend to my brother—and to me—that day. He went the extra mile and viewed my brother's body for me, which I found impossible to do at this dreadful time.

Later in the evening, I was back on the airplane headed home with all of the documents I needed in hand. Looking up into the heavens, I was thankful God had placed a special person in my brother's life, someone who stayed by his side and was there for him.

Instead of going to Oklahoma City to take the life of the person who had killed my brother, I had forgiven her. When I went to the police department, I found out Charlsie was claiming "self-defense." They inquired if I was okay with this plea or did I want to file charges against her. As I considered this, self-defense meant she wouldn't spend any time in prison—she wouldn't have to face a judge with charges of murder against her. It meant she would go free.

Could I deal with this? Who would care for her eight children? As my brother's closest of kin, I would become the trustee to distribute his government life insurance to each of his children until they reached eighteen years old. Should *she go free?* I remembered fourteen days before, when I stood guilty, as guilty as she could ever be. As I stood before the Judge of all of the earth, in heaven, He had forgiven me of all of my sins.

Remembering I had murdered many in my heart, I realized that she had murdered only one. I recall the truth, "If you say you love God and hate your brother, then you are the same as a murderer." I had hated many and He let me go free! I signed the papers; they approved my signature.

Later, in a tearful conversation with Charlsie, I expressed to her that I had forgiven her. With great remorse, she wept and thanked me for my kindness. This was my opportunity to lead her to the same Christ Who had forgiven me two weeks before.

When I returned home to Ft. Worth, I experienced one of the most heartrending days of my life. All of Dennis' children, who were there in the home when the gun was fired, came to the funeral. It became my duty to pick out the clothes, a casket, and a picture of my brother for the services, and write an obituary.

With my heart torn from my chest, like a mechanical robot, I was just going through the motions. The funeral home attendants were so helpful, but I was in a fog—hurting so deeply. It's almost impossible to explain it. The truth is that these times are worse than death because you have to walk through this nightmare alive. I tried to anticipate seeing my brother's body for the first time, trying to envision walking into the funeral home—entering the viewing room and looking at him. Reality set in; I knew I could talk to him, but he wouldn't hear me. I could reach to him, but he couldn't reach back to me. Death was so final—so painful and inescapable.

Where Dennis had gone after his death, I didn't know. It was impossible for me to know if he had made it to heaven, or if he hadn't. But I was not left without hope; surely somehow or someway, something had happened. I wanted to believe God had reached him. I was uncertain what I would do when I saw him. *Would I scream? Cry? Or faint? How would I react?*

Many people were at the funeral viewing area when I arrived. I looked down the long hall where the casket was. The walk seemed to last forever. *Could I make it?* On my left side were my wife, Barbara, and all of our daughters. Dennis' children were at the back of the room crying, along with my mom, dad, sister, and brother-in-law. All of the family had gathered there.

As I started toward the casket, my legs felt like they were going to collapse under me. I was never one who seemed to be weak but was always the strong one of the family. It was beyond my bereaved mind to imagine the pain I felt as I walked toward my brother's casket. I was so close to fainting. Panicking, I wanted to run, screaming, "I can't do this!" *Would this night-mare ever be over?* About five feet away from the casket, with my legs trembling violently, I heard a voice in my right ear that whispered to me, "He's in my presence." Stunned, I stopped for a moment and turned to look at who had stepped up beside me. *Who had walked up on my right side and spoken to me in my ear?* No one was there. I stood there—astonished.

How could this be? My brother had stopped attending church and lived a life in ways I knew would make it impossible for him to go to heaven. So how could it be that he was in God's presence? There are rules! And I knew the rules: you had to go to church, do the right things, have the right behaviors, and be faithful. He hadn't been. Dennis had walked away from the church and God's teachings years ago.

My mother had always held to the scripture, "Train up a child in the way he should go and when he is old he will not depart from it" (Prov. 22:6). *Could this scripture be coming true? Had this actually happened? Could God really rescue him in his last moments?*

Finally reaching the casket, I laid my hand on my brother's cold hand and looked into his face. At that moment, I knew he was at peace with God. The same peace came over me, the trembling stopped, and amazement overwhelmed me. I mumbled to myself, "How could he be in the presence of God?"

Quickly the story of the cross where the Lamb of God was crucified came to me. There were two thieves on each side of Jesus (Luke 23:32–43). One of them mocked, "If you really be the Son of God, bring yourself down and save us too." The other thief confessed, "We deserve what we have received, but He does not." To this Lamb of God he pled, "Remember me when you come into your kingdom."

The immediate response of Christ was, "Today, this day, you will be with me in paradise." Three or four seconds was all it took to acknowledge the sins he had committed, acknowledge Christ, who was hanging on the cross, and ask Him to remember him when He came into His kingdom. Just that quick! This repentant thief was forgiven while hanging on the cross.

This day he came to die for sins he had committed, but when he looked and beheld the Lamb of God, he received forgiveness. It doesn't take long once you acknowledge Him. Dennis had forty-five minutes. Wow! I wonder what must have gone on during that time, as he lay there in the presence of the faithful God—the God who had never left him but stayed with him to the very end of his time here on earth.

I couldn't be there, but God forgave, saved, and rescued my brother. Who else but God could do this? The psalmist wrote, "In the presence of God, there is fullness of joy and at His right hand there are pleasures forever more" (Ps. 16:11).

The next day was an interesting day as we laid my brother to rest. I looked around at the gravesites that one day would be mine and Barbara's. The grave of our second daughter, baby Charlotte, was nearby. I smiled as I thought of her awaiting our arrival in heaven one day. Fear and apprehension had left me; my legs weren't trembling anymore. There was no doubt the Comforter, the Holy Spirit, had come. As I walked away looking back, the voice spoke again, "He's in my presence."

We had bronze letters inscribed on his tombstone, "In His presence." I know that not only is he in His presence today, but Dennis is also experiencing the fullness of joy.

There is a God Who never leaves us, never gives up on us, never quits pursuing us, and loves us no matter how far we travel. His Holy Spirit is always close by, never leaving nor forsaking us. He is a God to Whom we can trust our eternal souls. There is simply no one else. God has proven Himself to be "a friend who sticks closer than a brother."

CHAPTER 4

THE CALL

There will always be critics. They fall into the category of skeptics, doubters, and those who just find it impossible to believe that something from the spiritual realm could happen to someone besides them. "After all," they say, "who are you, and what makes you so special?" They judge you and come to their own conclusions. I know—I was one—a critic, a judgmental person. The saddest part of all of this is that I had played all of the above roles. I remember the exhilarating feelings I experienced as I watched myself declaring and proclaiming from the supreme seat as a judge.

Everyone I brought into my jurisdiction met me in my own courtroom, and my personal judgment quickly found the person guilty of whatever I charged him or her with. But I was different now—everything had changed since I stood outside the throne room of the supreme God of creation. There I met the Judge of the whole earth, Who reserves the right to judge all humanity because He is the One Who made us.

God, my Judge, was so different from the way I thought He would be. He was full of mercy and grace as He forgave me of all my sins. As I told you earlier, it changed my life forever!

For two long and difficult days after my brother, Dennis, was buried, I was plagued with great bouts of insomnia and a seemingly never ending onslaught of voices in my head. Some seemed to be from God, others were possibly my own thoughts or from my enemy. There were many voices of people in my life doing their best to encourage me. Others told each other, "Oh, he's in shock." A few told my wife and family members, "The voices and visions will soon go away, leaving him embarrassed he ever told anyone these incredulous things."

Back when I sat high in my personal courtroom where I presided as judge of others, I had never even considered—or really even cared for—the feelings of those I judged outside of my immediate family. Now I knew the pain they must have felt—I allowed myself to experience it—all of it, until I reached a point of nausea and confusion.

I couldn't explain what was happening to me. It was difficult enough to convince myself, much less others, that I had gone to heaven, my sins were exposed on a transparent scroll, and God had forgiven me. It really stretches the imagination of everyone, including me.

Repeatedly, I asked myself, "Why are these things happening to me? Why would God show me these things?" It had to be God. I knew it was Him—there was no other explanation for the transformation that had occurred in me just weeks before my brother's murder. Wishing someone could sort out all of these events and give me some kind of sensible answers, I wondered, *Has anything similar to this ever happen to anyone before?*

The telephone beside my bed rang. It was early in the morning and I reluctantly reached to answer it. In my emotional and mental state, the last thing I wanted was to talk to anyone. I gathered myself as the caller quickly identified himself as a longtime acquaintance of mine. We exchanged cordial greetings, with my muddled mind drifting as he spoke. All of a sudden he said something that caught my ear.

"Listen, Alan. Early this morning, before the sun was even up, God woke me and told me to call you. He instructed me to tell you to read the story in Isaiah chapter six. It will give you the answers to what you're looking for."

Suddenly, upon hearing this statement, I was so startled that it caused me to jump up and sit on the side of the bed. Frightened, I wondered, *What is this I am hearing?* It was shocking enough to my emotions that I was hearing voices. Now God was waking someone else up in the darkness of the early morning to send me a message. Why would it be so urgent? Why in the world would God speak to me in the first place and now include another person and tell him to call me with a chapter and verse in Isaiah I was not familiar with? How could this be the answer to the questions I had sought?

All the voices, the tragic murder of my brother, burying him in the cold, wet ground in January—was almost more than I could bear. The most pressing thing to me was not to know what Isaiah would have to say concerning me at this present time.

It was impossible to get a grip in my mind on how this would be the answers to my private questions. Trying to conceal my amazement with uncertain politeness, I said, "Mike, thank you for calling and sharing this with me, but I will need to talk to you at a later time." In my weary mind, I was still trying to grasp the mystery of God speaking to me, much less this person who had called. Would God actually speak to another person with answers to the questions I was asking?

Traveling to Lewisville to meet with my job superintendent, Danny, took up the majority of my day. He was much more than an employee. He was my trusted friend and a person I could confide in.

Following the meeting, I returned home and shared dinner with my wife and daughters. Barbara inquired, "Honey, do you remember what chapter and verse in the Bible it was that Mike left with you this morning, that you were supposed to read?"

My reply came hesitatingly, trying to remember . . . "Isaiah chapter six." She went to the bookshelf and found my dusty, black Bible—the one with my name engraved on its front cover. She had given it to me some years earlier with the hopes one day I would take time to read it.

Six hours had passed before I opened the Bible and searched for the book named Isaiah. *Surely it must be somewhere in the Old Testament,* I pondered. Though I had attended church all my life, I was not a student of the Holy Scriptures, especially the Old Testament. My fingers flipped back and forth through the pages of my Bible until I finally found it. I began to read in Isaiah 6:

> In the year that King Uzziah died, I saw the Lord seated on a throne, high and exalted, and the train of his robe filled the temple. Above him were seraphs, each with six wings: With two wings they covered their faces, with two they covered their feet, and with two they were

flying. And they were calling to one another: "Holy, holy, holy is the Lord Almighty; The whole earth is full of his glory." At the sound of their voices the doorposts and thresholds shook and the temple was filled with smoke. "Woe to me!" I cried. "I am undone! For I am a man of unclean lips, and I live among a people of unclean lips, and my eyes have seen the King, the Lord Almighty." Then one of the seraphs flew to me with a live coal in his hand, which he had taken with tongs from the altar. With it he touched my mouth and said, "See, this has touched your lips; your guilt is taken away and your sin atoned for."

Verse eight says, "Then I heard the voice of the Lord saying, 'Whom shall I send? And who will go for us?' And I said, 'Here am I, send me!'"

As I read verse eight, I heard a whisper rise up from the depths of my soul, and I joined Isaiah, saying, "Here I am, send me!" Surprisingly, I understood. An unexplainable joy swelled up inside of me. At last I knew of someone besides me who had been carried into heaven and returned.

Isaiah had stood at the throne of God and seen the smoke—the same smoke I had seen. He had admitted that he, too, was unworthy and unclean. But the greatest thing I discovered—the greatest thing of all—was that though he was guilty of many sins, yet God loved him and forgave him of them all. This prophet's experience touched my soul. I rejoiced in the fact that Isaiah's sins were washed away—and so were mine.

My sins were really forgiven! My transgressions—every wrongdoing, every offense, every little indiscretion—all my iniquities were gone. I was completely freed by the mercies of my loving God!

With renewed energy and determination, I declared again, "Here I am, send me! Whatever You tell me to do, I will do it. The words You speak to me, I will repeat without fear of rebuke or reprisal. I will go where You want me to go." I turned my eyes toward the heavens and with a grateful heart exclaimed, "Thank You, God."

Breathing deeply—to relieve all the anxiety that had built up inside of me, at last I was certain God would provide an answer to every question and would fulfill all of them at the right time. His purpose through me would be accomplished as long as I was willing to obey Him.

My heart was full of adoration, and joy grew deep in my being, knowing God knew me before I was ever born, and He had determined what role I would play here on earth. His plans for me would be good plans, although some of them might be difficult for me to understand or fulfill.

I, too, had learned, as Isaiah did, that obedience to God was to become my most difficult endeavor but would develop into my greatest virtue. Isaiah's vision was his call to be God's messenger to tell those who would believe that they were blessed by God—that this same God was going to destroy them because of their disobedience.

Here I was, once a Pharisee full of lofty pride who, out of anger, had judged and passed judgment on others. I had been wounding and unforgiving, pretending I loved God and hating so many others. God's love transformed and changed me, and now He would send me with this same message to those who were so much like me to convince them to become familiar with His voice, repent of their sins, and serve the one and only true God and His Son, Jesus Christ.

The awesomeness of His greatness, mystery, and power caused me to recognize my sinfulness and desire His forgiveness. When I confessed my sins, He empowered me to be the man and the conqueror He had called me to be.

CHAPTER 5

SONG IN THE NIGHT

Everything I have ever done has been with all of my might, full speed ahead. Every finger has been broken—one has been re-attached, both shoulders separated, one knee destroyed and re-built, cuts and stitches endured, and every conceivable injury by football, skiing, nail guns, and saws of all kinds. My mother said I was injury prone after having been to an emergency room five times before my twelfth birthday. To me, pain is just for a moment.

Everything concerning me heals faster than for most people. One day it's a cut, and then seemingly the next day the wound has turned into a scar. But today I'm finding myself much more vulnerable than in my past. I'm coming to grips with the truth that I'm no longer a superior human, able to solve my problems and find an answer to dilemmas in my life. My need for help from someone greater than myself is my only hope of surviving the difficulties of life.

The last great enemy called death has shown me no mercy, with the onslaught of voices accusing me, as if it were my fault that my brother, Dennis, died. Feelings of distress kept washing over me like the waves of the sea, as if they had a mission to drown me in grief. Continuously, these feelings marched unrelenting through my entire being.

My demoralizing enemy laid to waste my reputation as a pillar of strength. I screamed and hollered from the top of my lungs, "Shut up! Shut up! You liar!"

Undaunted, the accuser repeated, "If only you had done" this or "if you had done" that. If you had only been there, you could have saved him. The voices played violently with my mind and my emotions. A video of me arriving at Dennis' house, running up the steps, bursting through the open door, and diving in front of my brother as the gun is fired played. I watched myself take the bullet into my chest—in his place—rescuing him from death over and over again.

Never have I had a greater desire or need for the Living God to be close to me than I did then. With my personality, I have always been quick to face my problems and confront my enemy. The faster I stepped up to the plate and swung at the first pitch, the sooner whatever I was battling was over.

Have you ever had a recurring dream? I dreamed and dreamed again I was being pursued by something or someone *big*—bigger than myself. And even though I ran with all my might, he was overtaking me. As he reached to grab me, I began to rise into the air. The more I waved my arms, the higher I flew. I was like a bird, flying above the mountains, leaving the valleys far behind. The higher I flew, the smaller my troubles became and the one pursing me diminished into nothingness.

One morning, I came crashing to earth when I realized it had been seven sad and lonely days since my brother was placed into the cold, frozen ground in Bluebonnet Cemetery. The certainty of knowing chilled me. Realizing he no longer walked the earth sat on top of me like a stone wall. All the good times we shared were over!

No more Dairy Queen. He would never be there again to take the first lick. The two of us running and playing kick-the-can, hide and seek, or red rover, red rover, let Dennis come over . . .

Never again the thrill of two freckled-faced boys sleeping together and hearing strange sounds in the nighttime, pulling the covers up over our heads and lying as flat as we could so we would not be found by the bogey man we visualized had entered through our window. Only the memories remain—I am running like the wind. My big brother has sent me on a deep-and-out pattern, with me looking over my shoulder, trying to catch the spiraling football. It's a touchdown all the way! He runs down the field to the goal line and we meet in mid-air with high fives. Embracing each other as we tumble to the turf, we roll across the field in celebration.

Yes! Those were the days! Right now, if given the opportunity, I would gladly, in the middle of the night, go to every bar or jail he might be imprisoned in to look for him endlessly until I found him. It would be my greatest thrill to rescue him, look on his handsome face, into the depths of his blue eyes, grab him, and hold him just one more time. This time I would never let him go. But I knew . . . there would be no new memories with my brother.

The voice of God has assured me, comforted me, and seemed to stay close to me most of the time during all the grief. Still, the pain and aching in my heart and feelings of loneliness did not subside.

I returned to my construction company and focused on the task at hand, building block enclosures for dogs at Tooth Acre Kennels. As I stepped out of my truck near the construction site, the smells coming from the dog pens hit me hard in the face. The blustering winds and gloom from the dark and dreary clouds hanging close overhead seemed to envelop my whole world.

As I turned my eyes toward the sky, wishing rain would come so I could go home and hide from it all, the dogs were not barking. It was quiet and still for a short time. In the distance, one dog began to howl, then another, and then another. More than fifty dogs howled. The more they howled, the more the mountain of mourning began to build up inside me. I wanted to go somewhere and cry and cry until I washed all the pain inside me out into the damp dirt packed down at the construction site.

Grief was taking its toll. Agony had stolen my appetite, leaving me with very little motivation to go on in life. After eight hours of stormy weather and howling dogs, my heart still ached. I wondered, *Will this pain ever be completely gone?*

Emotionally exhausted, I arrived home at sunset after a long, hard day. Barbara had prepared a wonderful dinner and it was ready to be served. Sitting around the table, my three daughters, Taleesa, Tamara, and Tricia all looked at me with their big brown eyes full of love and concern. I looked at each of them and then at Barbara. With a heart full of pain, I took her into my arms and kissed her.

"Honey," she inquired, "are you okay?"

Looking away toward an open door, I murmured, "It's been a very difficult day." I sat down to the table, confiding, "I'm glad it's over now that I'm home."

After dinner I took time to be with all three of my girls. We laughed and listened to each one tell stories about her school day. I helped Taleesa to better understand the metric system; she would be having a test on Friday. Tamara had a science project only Daddy could design and build. Tricia's was simpler. All she needed was for Daddy to repair the arm of a broken doll.

Barbara had helped me learn that the most important thing in life was our family. Some months before, I had made arrangements, paid the fees, and entered our championship softball team into a league for the coming season. We had ordered new uniforms, purchased new equipment, and were preparing for another championship season. She sat down in my office and reminded me that our three daughters were growing up fast, and the time we had left should be spent with them. She asked me to consider giving up my softball team.

Tenderly, she left my office with these words, "I know you love our girls more than anything, and you will do the right thing."

It was not what she said, but what she didn't say that left me in deep thought. To be all I could be for my daughters meant I would have to give up my pursuits of being a professional bass fisherman, a dream I had harbored in my heart many times. I would have to surrender my championship softball team into the hands of someone else. These decisions, which I had not considered before, were now displayed before my eyes. Alone, I weighed my pursuits against my love for my wife and my three daughters. *Whom or what did I love the most? Which one meant more to me?*

Within five minutes, I made three phone calls, giving my softball team and all the new equipment, including uniforms, to someone else. Within weeks, I sold my treasured bass rig and threw that old pigskin football into the corner. This freed me to spend all my time with the greatest treasure of my life, my family!

My daughters always had this idea that Daddy could fix anything. Little did they know there was one thing I couldn't fix—my own broken heart.

When it was finally time for bed, I hugged and held each one. Their prayers were said, nightlights turned on, and everyone tucked in tight with reassuring words, "Sweet dreams, I'll see you in the morning. I love you!"

Sliding into bed with the woman I love and adore, I was still so sad and lonely. I reached up and turned off the lamp and then stared into the darkness, focused on the ceiling. I wished somehow I could turn off my thoughts and memories like a lamp. I needed to do something—anything—to make the pain in my heart go away.

The storm had passed. Its thundering stopped and the lighting ceased. Only the stillness, quietness, and loneliness remained—filling the room.

Then I heard something. I rose from my pillow and looked toward Barbara. In the darkness I asked her, "Do you hear what I hear?"

"I hear a songbird singing," she whispered. The two of us pushed ourselves up gently to a sitting position and leaned back softly against the head of our bed so we wouldn't disturb our night visitor. We listened with great intensity, as if to fine tune our ears to the night singer so we might identify its origin, as he sung his song just outside our window.

Barbara reached over and gently took my hand, sliding her fingers between mine. She quietly asked, "Is it a whippoorwill?"

Reaching back into my memory of years gone by, I recalled the song of the night singer who repeats his name over and over again. *Whip-poor-will, whip-poor-will, whip-poor-will.*

This was not the ancestry of the vocalist we were hearing. I gently touched her on the arm and whispered softly, "No, it is not a whippoorwill."

She replied, "The crisp and clear notes are so vocal you can all but hear the words."

We sat there holding hands, allowing tears to wash away our grief as our serenader, sent from our heavenly Father, complimentary of His amazing love, sweetly sang as every note fell gently into our spirits, soothing us, healing us, and restoring our broken hearts.

Our grief began to dissipate as the joy began to return. Peace once again flowed in us, forming new scars on our wounds. God had sent a gift from heaven in the form of a songbird. With the comfort of His song, my broken heart was mending and the pain was lifting. My long night was passing. I went to sleep with a smile on my face. I was confident the morning would bring joy once again into the depths of my being.

As I awoke, it was as I had hoped. Peace and joy flowed like a river as I headed off to work at the construction site. Sure enough the dogs were barking and yelping, but it didn't matter to me anymore. The song in the night gave me one of the best days since my brother had gone away.

God had sent a comforter to me in the form of a songbird. His was a beautiful song of peace, joy, and healing. My long night had truly ended and my morning had come!

It must not have been much different when Mary Magdalene showed up at the tomb on the Sabbath morning after Christ had been crucified. She came to mourn and be close to her Savior. As she wept, an angel came and asked her, "Why seek you the living among the dead?" She ran to tell the disciples, "He's not there; He is risen."

This is the way it is for all of those who die in Christ. Only their bodies are in the grave. The essence of who they are has ascended safely into His arms. Together with Him, they are enjoying all the greatness and splendor of heaven. In His presence, there is no more sorrow, tears, or dying, for the former things have passed away.

My world had been turned upside down as God's world came to the forefront of my life. I had been one who studied, like a religion, the art of topographic fishing, which refers to the contour of the land before it is flooded to become a lake, who spent every waking moment perfecting plays for my beloved football teams and practicing endlessly with my commercial softball team. Now my love for these was consumed in moments as I stood in the presence of the transforming God. I could not be satisfied with those pursuits ever again.

With my newfound hunger for the Scriptures, I plunged with all of my mind and soul into the depths of the all-consuming God, to learn of Him and do whatever He asked me to do.

I would be available for Him at all times, for the One who is in all things my Comforter, my Savior, and my greatest Friend. "Deep calls to deep, in the roar of your waterfalls, all your waves and breakers have swept over me. By day the Lord directs His love, at night His song is with me—a prayer to the God of my life" (Ps. 42:7–8 NIV).

CHAPTER 6

OBEDIENCE

I loved and revered my mother. She was a woman of faith, one who feared God. If there ever really was a saint, she was one. My obedience to her never was a problem because I loved and respected her. As a young man, I was amazed by how people in authority—coaches, teachers, fathers of the girls I dated, and one day the military—by position or self-appointment tried to force their will on me. Their approaches, their attitudes, or just the way they spoke gave me all the fuel I needed to begin my rebellion against authority.

My position was simply, *Who are you to tell me what to do?* If I knew you didn't love me and showed disrespect toward me, the result included a major conflict. And even though my life had changed greatly since my trip to the throne room, I still held tight to these "virtues."

Two months had passed since I lost my brother, Dennis. Things were better. The wounds from my loss were not red anymore but were turning white into scars. The Comforter had performed an incredible work in me. The Great Physician, Jesus, with the skills only He possesses, had carefully pieced back together the fragments of my broken heart. Trying to understand why He cared so deeply for me staggered my imagination. It was not just knowing He died on an old rugged cross for the sins of all mankind so long ago that awed me, but also understanding that He, the mighty God, still lives today and makes us—fallen humanity—the object of His affection.

Reality began to overwhelm me. I had fallen in love with the Lord God of all creation and He had become my greatest friend. To love, honor, and obey Him had become my most compelling motivation, not only in this world, but also in the one to come.

I was focused, working on a new home in Lewisville, Texas. Danny Ratliff, a longtime employee and trusted friend, was by my side. I personally trained him in the construction business. His willingness to learn and desire to excel in life and the trades made him undeniably one of the finest employees I have ever had. A heavy overcast sky with its occasional scattered thunderstorms had driven us inside to work, out of the falling rain. The weather conditions forced the decision that Danny and I would build a fireplace in the corner of the large, ranch-style family room. It was a dreary, early spring morning as Danny carried out his job meticulously, as usual.

Yet I couldn't help but notice his demeanor was seemingly very troubled. At first, I pushed it from my mind, blaming the look on his face on the inclement weather conditions. Observing Danny further, my concerns grew.

Knowing he was a very sensitive person, I approached him gently and, nudging him, I said, "Danny, why are you so sad this morning?"

Slowly, he began, "You remember a few weeks ago I told you Marilyn had been critically injured in an automobile accident, and among her serious injuries were two broken and crushed legs."

I listened intently, fearing her condition had become worse. Danny continued, "Tomorrow they are scheduled to amputate at least one of her legs. The family, including myself, has prayed, asking God to perform a miracle on her behalf, believing God still heals and restores." He paused, looked across the room with tears in His eyes, and said hesitantly, "I guess He's not going to."

At that moment, it happened. I heard a voice speaking audibly in my right ear, giving me details and instructions I was to obey and carry out on behalf of the one who spoke. God was listening to our conversation!

The words were crisp and clear: "Tonight I want you to go to Harris Hospital to deliver a message for me." I froze and held my breath for a few seconds. I could hardly move. *What in the world is this all about?* I couldn't understand what I was hearing. *Why me?*

As the voice continued to give me instructions, I was somewhat relieved that He gave me the bad news first. What He said to me next seemed in some ways ridiculous. "I want you to go now to a florist and buy a bouquet of lilies and make certain they will be delivered to Marilyn's room no later than five o'clock P.M."

No wonder my head was spinning. Was this voice telling me to leave my job, with dirty work clothes on, and go immediately to a flower shop and purchase a bouquet of lilies for another woman?

Then the voice whispered, "The lilies will let her know you are coming. Remind her I am the Lily of the Valley. Then inform her that she will walk out of this valley on her own two feet."

Stunned, I gathered my strength and walked to my truck to sort this thing out. It sounded insane. Opening the door, I slid into the seat, placing my arms on the steering wheel with my head on my arms, trying to compose myself. I shut my eyes tight and began to recall five years earlier when we had left a church I had been a part of for twenty-eight years.

The circumstances were extremely difficult. Sadly, the senior pastor was wounded by the events that had occurred under his watch. My respect and admiration for this unique and interesting man suffered greatly. I felt angry and bitter toward many of my church acquaintances during this difficult time. The church split because of the turmoil, causing the senior pastor to resign on this own volition. My family and approximately sixty others left the church under the guidance of a new pastor, starting a new congregation.

Those were days of anger, bitterness, and hatred, putting on the acts of righteousness, not realizing they were the deeds of hypocrites. Thank God, He had carried me into heaven and revealed to me what I was, forgave me, and changed me into a new person. Those old voices no longer ruled my life.

The former pastor of the church we had left and his wife were traveling to the hills of South Dakota to visit Marilyn's parents. James, a noted teacher of end-time prophecy, had scheduled meetings at local churches in the nearby cities where their family lived. Tragically, late one night on a dark, lonely highway, rounding a curve, the oncoming headlights of a speeding automobile crossed the median, blinding James. It caused him to lose control of his automobile. He veered off the road into a ravine and crashed head-on into an embankment.

Marilyn was pinned beneath the wreckage. With feelings of helplessness, James called upon the only One he knew Who could hear him and would surely respond to his cries. "Jesus, save us. Oh, God, help us!"

It seemed like an eternity before help finally arrived to extract the mangled and broken body of his beloved wife from the wreckage. With only faint signs of life still remaining, she was rushed to the nearest hospital, a small rural facility.

Upon arrival, the emergency team administered the necessary treatment to stabilize her condition, saving her life. Finally, taking the X-rays of her badly crushed legs, the doctors were not prepared for what they saw. It looked as if someone had slammed a hard-boiled egg against the concrete, shattering its shell into dozens of pieces.

To reset and repair the bones would be impossible. The only alternative, to save her life, would be amputation. This decision seemed to be a devastating certainty.

James, after a period of time, returned home to Ft. Worth to make arrangements for his wife to be flown to Harris Hospital. There she would be placed into the qualified hands of specialized physicians, hoping to not only preserve her life, but to save one or both of her legs.

Even though I personally had not seen nor been in contact with James and Marilyn for more than five years, I had remained in contact with a few of their friends, who related the news of this traumatic accident to me.

They had two sons, Bobby and Ricky. The oldest one, Bobby, was one of Danny's best friends. The three of us played football on an intercity championship team. Because of the position I had taken in the church split, Bobby was deeply wounded and became angry and bitter toward me. Danny shared with me the statement Bobby had made to him—"If I ever see Alan Youngblood again, I'll kill him."

Now, hearing the voice of God, recalling these memories, and knowing I needed to do what God had asked of me, left me shaken. I blew the horn on my truck for Danny to go to lunch. As we drove down the road, I told him what had happened. As I spoke, I imagined he thought I was losing my mind. *Hearing voices! Taking orders from someone unseen!*

As we left the restaurant, I continued to share with Danny. I was told to "Go to a florist and order a bouquet of lilies for Marilyn and send them ahead. This would prepare the way for my coming." The nearest florist was Gordon Boswell in Lewisville.

As we opened the door, a small bell rang and a young woman came from a back room. There we stood—two construction workers with caps on our heads, wearing work boots, T-shirts, and dirty blue jeans. She must have wondered what we were doing in a florist shop. Her warm greeting, "May I help you?" was followed by my weak reply as my eyes searched, trying to see if they had any lilies.

I was certain, after this voice had given me clear instructions of what to do, that the lilies would be there waiting for me. My problem was I didn't know what a lily even looked like. A rose, carnation, or orchid I was more familiar with. I looked up at her and said, "Do you have any lilies?" I felt like an idiot in front of Danny, asking for these flowers.

She cordially replied, "I'm sorry, but it's too early for lilies. Check back in a week to ten days and they will be in. It's too early for them now."

My face must have turned crimson red; I was horribly embarrassed. *I have made a fool of myself!* The telephone behind the counter began to ring, giving us an opportunity to get out of there. Danny beat me to the door with the little bell ringing. I hurried after him. I wanted to escape.

Then I heard the voice of the shopkeeper behind me saying, "Sir, wait just a minute."

I didn't want to wait, not even another second! Danny held the door open and I looked at him then looked to her. She smiled. "You will not believe this. It was another one of our stores calling from Ft. Worth, Texas. She was calling to tell me they had just received an order of lilies at their store, and they have a large supply for any of my customers."

Stunned, I returned to the counter and asked her where this store was located. To my surprise, the store was only half a block from Harris Hospital. I quickly took out my credit card and asked if I could pay for the lilies here and the other Gordon Boswell shop could deliver them for me. I needed them delivered before 5:00 P.M. She assured me they would be delivered today. I took a deep breath as I scribbled by name on the credit card receipt, making sure a small card with my name on it would be attached to the bouquet of lilies.

Danny and I hardly spoke on our return to the job site. We were both amazed by the events that had occurred. Now all I had to do was go home and convince Barbara that she and I, by 7:30 P.M., needed to drive to Harris Hospital, catch an elevator, walk into a room full of people we hadn't seen in five years, and deliver a message.

Before my life was changed, I never wanted to see these people again. But now all had changed. I had to deliver a message to Marilyn. "He is the Lily of the Valley, God is with her, and she will walk out of this valley on her own two feet."

I am not a fearful person, seldom ever afraid of anything, never getting nervous, but this night I was sweating profusely as I walked out of the hospital elevator.

The door to Marilyn's hospital room stood open. Peeking inside, I saw it packed with more than twenty people. At the far end of the room, on the window sill, sat Bobby. As Barbara and I entered, every voice hushed and all eyes fell sharply on us. I ignored their faces—looking at the shelves that lined the wall, overflowing with flowers everywhere.

About to panic, I turned to Barbara and asked, "Do you see the lilies?"

"Yes, honey. They're here," she whispered.

Bobby quickly stood up and made his way toward me. A hush came over the room as every person watched in fear of what might happen. I let my eyes lock on his with my muscles tense and ready. He reached me quickly. His right hand, wide open, extended toward me. It was not a fist, but a welcoming handshake. We embraced, and in my right ear he said, "I love you."

"I love you, too," I said. And I meant it.

Now the time had come for me to carry out my instructions. I turned toward the hospital bed, took a few steps, and leaned over close to Marilyn. She spoke first. "Alan, thank you for the lilies. I knew you would be coming."

My throat was tight and I choked up as I delivered my assignment. "Marilyn, He told me to remind you He is the Lily of the Valley and you will walk out of this valley on your own two feet." *Wow! I did it! Relief!*

Though it was difficult to obey God and be His messenger, still it gave me the greatest joy I had ever experienced. Pleasing Him instead of myself would become my greatest endeavor for the rest of my life. Jubilant, I grabbed Barbara by the hand, waved good-bye to everyone, and smiled as we walked out of the room much faster than we had entered. We walked across the parking lot, hand in hand, beaming, and floating as if on air. We were both glad this was over.

Obedience to God was the hardest thing I had ever done. I hoped we had passed the test. I felt certain that this was only the beginning of our walk. Hopefully, we had carried out what He had instructed us to do. The rest was up to Him.

Five days later on a Sunday morning at our church, one of the ladies who had been visiting the hospital came to me and asked, "Have you heard about Marilyn?" I looked at her quizzically. She could tell by my reaction I didn't have any idea what she was speaking of. She continued, "The next morning after your visit they were scheduled to remove at least one of her legs. The doctors decided to do one last X-ray to make certain there was no other option. When they did the X-ray, they couldn't believe their eyes. They said an accelerated healing process was well under way and amputation was no longer necessary."

I was informed that Marilyn left the hospital in about three weeks, but it was quite some time before I was able to see her. The months would come and go before Barbara and I finally did see her. There she was, with James lovingly close by her side, walking into a large cafeteria on a Sunday afternoon.

At last, before my very eyes, I saw her walking without the assistance of even a cane. There was no sign of the traumatic accident that had not claimed her life and could not take her legs! She had walked out of the valley on her own two feet!

I recalled words from First Samuel 15:22, "Obedience is far better than sacrifice." There are times we, being human, feel we are doing what God wants of us by going to church every time the doors are open, sacrificially giving our money to help the poor and needy, buying seating for the church sanctuary, or working on a Saturday church project. In our minds we are content thinking we have given sacrificially of ourselves. Surely this has impressed God!

But I have learned that one simple act of obedience, though it be challenging or places us into an uncomfortable situation, is far greater than all the sacrifices we could ever give.

When you carry out obedience to God, this allows you to walk from a physical world into His supernatural realm where all things become possible for those who believe.

CHAPTER 7

THE CLOTHES

So many visions! It's like the drifting snow clouds in a Colorado winter. Voices, like the sounds of many waterfalls of Niagara, and miracles, too many to tell about, continue even as we met at the home of our close friends, David and Linda Gregg on a November night. They had invited between fifty and sixty guests for pot luck dinner and fellowship, and they asked me to speak.

As I walked throughout the grounds and from room to room of their large home, I observed some of the guests who were gathered there: Des Evans, the senior pastor of a large local church, Mike Evans, an international Jewish speaker, Ben Martin, one of my mentors, and many faces from my past. Then I spotted a familiar face I didn't expect to see. *Oh, no! Surely not her,* I thought.

I moved quickly to the back patio and looked up toward the stars, attempting to gather my thoughts of what to do. Earlier, my friend Ben Martin had pulled me aside and told me God had impressed him to have me share the encounter of being carried into heaven and seeing Jerry Hardgrave at the throne of God. This wasn't what I had intended to share. In the past eleven months I had told this story to hundreds of people in churches and groups of various kinds. Many wonderful things continued to happen. But because Ben had requested this particular experience, I reluctantly consented.

But when I saw Cheryl, a school teacher, I was hesitant to follow through on Ben's request. I had heard the stories of the long, dark midnight that Jerry's wife, Cheryl, had been living in for the past two or three years since her husband's plane had crashed in the mountains of Mexico. I did not want to inflict any more pain on this precious woman. Enough is enough! The stories told of raging fear and unrelenting voices that were driving her to the edge of insanity, creating concern on the part of loved ones and friends who feared she would lose her mind. The thoughts of Jerry surviving the plane crash and being lost somewhere in the mountains of Mexico and wandering around trying to find his way back home had driven her to travel to the remote villages and the very mountainside where the mangled, burnt wreckage of the plane remained.

Trembling, she had shown his photograph to many, asking if they had seen this man. She was tormented, spending sleepless nights haunted by nightmare after nightmare, driven by a lying voice repeatedly telling her, "Jerry is not in heaven, nor in hell. There is no soul! When we die," the voice declared, "we are no different from a dog." Taunting Cheryl, the voice continued, "You will never see him again because there is no life after death!"

The snide and cutting voices came from the bowels of hell; wave after wave, trying to steal her sanity. The spirit of fear has no mercy. These lying demons will one day be chained and thrown into the lake of fire, finally meeting their end!

The revelation of all Cheryl was dealing with engulfed my whole being. I realized she needed to hear what I had seen and experienced eleven months ago. I left the patio and entered through the open door, where I came into a large round family room. There all the guests had gathered; all were seated or standing around the room. In the center was a chair like a barstool for me to sit on, so all could hear the story of the clothes that would change the world of one woman who had been tormented night and day.

As I shared my story about Jerry on many occasions, people asked me if I knew why he was wearing the clothes his mother-in-law had made, with matching tie and penny loafers. I told them that each and every detail concerning my vision of heaven had been fulfilled except the clothes. Over and over, listeners said, "The Bible says we shall be known as we are known." I assured them I didn't think this was the reason I saw Jerry in these unique clothes.

I would have known Jerry no matter what he had been wearing. I knew Him because I recognized his face—wrinkle free, peaceful, smiling, and better-looking than ever. I believed one day God would reveal the meaning of Jerry's clothes to me.

Before I took my seat on the stool, I pulled David close to me and asked if Cheryl knew about the story of heaven and her husband, Jerry. David whispered, "No. She hasn't heard the story and doesn't know anything about it."

Sitting on the stool, as my eyes circled the room, I spotted Cheryl seated with her oldest daughter, Jerri, sitting next to her. She looked so tired; her eyes were hollow, her mouth drawn, and her black hair was turning white. Grief had taken its toll on this innocent woman.

I began to tell one more time of the encounter that changed my life. I turned on the stool toward Cheryl and related each detail while looking at her face. Finally, I came to the part about Jerry sitting on the bottom step of the throne in heaven. I could see the soul of a troubled woman. Looking in her eyes with great compassion and the care of a physician, I spoke directly to her, "Cheryl, the man sitting on the bottom step was Jerry."

Instantly, her eyes enlarged and I heard her gasp. As I continued, she grasped her daughter's arm. I said, "It was strange. Jerry did not have on a white robe, but instead he wore a suit of clothes I had seen him wear previously one Easter Sunday, ten years ago. The coat was dark blue and white tweed and the pants were dark blue. He had on a matching double-knit tie, just like the suit. He was wearing penny loafer shoes." Cheryl was shaking. I looked directly at her and said, "Cheryl, it was the suit your mother made for him!"

I grabbed the edge of the stool as she stood up. With a gasping voice she pleaded, "May I say something?" I didn't know what she was going to do or say, but I nodded my head, signaling her to go ahead.

Weeping, she began, "I have experienced a long, terrible siege of nightmares and pain. I have wrestled with an agony because I would never see Jerry again. Just . . . fighting horrible thoughts that he no longer existed." She choked over her words as she struggled to speak. "It has been impossible for me to let him go. I knew Jerry's remains were in a body bag, burned beyond recognition." She paused, wiping her eyes, barely able to continue, "The night before the funeral, I found it impossible to live with the agonizing thought of Jerry being buried naked, forever without any clothes on. In the middle of the night, I secretly went to the closet where all of his suits hung and slowly looked at them one by one, touching them—remembering the handsome man who wore these clothes.

"These beautiful suits were looking back at me. Then, there it was at the back of the closet, hanging there all these years, completely out of sight. I reached back and carefully lifted his most loved suit from the closet. My mind went back to that Easter Sunday morning so very long ago; the double-knit blue and white tweed coat with matching tie, and dark blue pants." She laughed through her tears, "It was his favorite suit.

"I called Jerry Lucas, the owner of Lucas Funeral Home, and asked him to meet me shortly after midnight. I firmly expressed to him, 'This meeting has to be completely confidential.' I didn't want anyone to know what I had done! Early in the morning, in the darkness, we met at a private back door. In my arms, I carried my secret treasure—these clothes—covered by a dark plastic bag. I made Jerry Lucas promise again, never to tell anyone our hidden secret. I could not bear the thought of Jerry being buried without clothes on. I thrust the clothes toward him and said, 'Put the suit on him, and the shirt, and by all means, the tie. Drape it around his neck. Place the shoes at his feet inside his casket.'"

Finishing the rest of my story seemed irrelevant compared to hers. All around the room, everywhere I looked, people were wiping their eyes. She said, as she finished her story, "I have never told anyone my secret. I was afraid that people would think I was certainly losing my mind."

I stood up, shaken but greatly relieved. Tears rolled down my face because I had an overwhelming reality of a God Who would look down from heaven and use someone like me to let

Cheryl know Jerry was alive and having a wonderful time in God's heaven. God freed her from the grasp of the despicable evil spirit called fear, which had terrorized and assaulted her unrelentingly for too many years. The enemy had taken her life and slammed it against the rocks, shattering it into a thousand pieces.

But this night she yielded to the Potter, the one who had made her. He reached down and picked up the pieces, and using all but one, molded her and made her new again. He healed and restored, giving her the pursuit of happiness so she could once again enjoy life with her daughters and their families. Cheryl thrived with new life, returning to the classroom and one memorable day she found a new love and surrendered her hand in marriage.

The remaining years of her life on earth were a melody of praise for the God Who had made her. Quickly, too quickly, she left this veil of tears and entered into the joys of heaven. I can almost see her as she walked through the gates of the celestial city, looking for a specific man, the one with the face all aglow and wearing the suit her mother had made. She knew exactly where he would be waiting!

I am certain that he was not sitting on the bottom step on the beautiful, marble platform, but was standing in anticipation with his arms outstretched and opened wide to receive his beloved. At this moment of their embrace, at last, I believe she held in her arms the missing piece. Then and only then was she made completely whole!

When Cheryl's mother, so many years before, had sat down in front of her Singer sewing machine and lovingly fashioned the unique double-knit suit with the matching coat and tie, I wonder if she could have imagined that one day this same handmade suit would become "evidence of life after death," completely healing her beloved daughter.

If so, she could not have known that just a mortal man like me would be translated into heaven, see Jerry Hardgrave wearing the same suit of clothes, and then return with undeniable proof that would defy the logic of all skeptics and unbelievers.

This "irrefutable evidence" of life after death will bring hope, enlighten the mind, and change the lives of all those who will believe! "Now faith is being sure of what we hope for and certain of what we do not see" (Heb. 11:1 NIV).

CHAPTER 8

SILENCE

O, God, do not keep silent, be not quiet, O God.
Be not still.

—Psalm 83:1 NIV

I stumbled down the stairway into the deserted hallway of my home. Looking out a window as I groped my way toward my study, I could see that the sky was still pitch black, without even one ray of light.

With the world still asleep, I felt so alone. Hopefully, the morning would soon come. Desperately needing a new day to dawn, I would gladly exchange these voices of my worst nightmare that continually haunt me, for the noises of a busy day.

Thoughts invading my mind in the nighttime had reached a crescendo, banging in my head like drums and clanging cymbals. Their rumbling, troubling voices were causing me to have vertigo, with my head spinning. Thoughts of hopelessness left me in despair, with fear racing through my head like a herd of wild buffalo on a lonely Texas plain.

At last I reached the doorway of my study, sliding my clammy hand across the wall to locate the light switch in the darkened room. As the light illuminated my office, my eyes located my Bible. I knew within its pages lay my only hope!

Sitting down in my desk chair, I began to turn its hallowed pages in search of a word, possibly a scripture that would assure me God had not left me. In my despair, I had sought God and found Him not. I had searched high and low, screaming, "Where are You, God? Have You left me? Why are You not speaking to me any more? Or is it I have gone deaf?"

I heard nothing but the echo of my voice with no reply. It was as if God had become mute! The vastness of His silence stifled me to the point of complete desperation as I tried to find something to soothe my troubled soul.

Seated there behind my desk with my Bible in my hand, desperately I cried out to God. "Don't remain silent! Don't allow my enemies to triumph over me. Come to my rescue, O God. Don't take Your holy presence from me."

Silence.

All that seemed left was hope; hope in a God Who appeared to have forgotten me. No matter the test, nor the severity of my trials, my heart must go on trusting in God and His promises despite the absence of His presence during my dark and fearful times.

Asking as Jesus asked His Father, "Why, O God, have You forsaken me?"

I felt alone except for the voices in my head, which were trying to overwhelm me. As they continued their onslaught, I wondered aloud, "Why do these troubles continue? God, where are You? I don't know how long it has been since You have spoken to me. Did You go away? If You did go away, then why?" Growing frantic and speaking out loud again I continued, "God, You of all people should understand how difficult it is to be a human with all of the situations which come into our lives, the troubles, the problems, the loneliness, the scary times. You have suffered every one of these. For me to have to suffer the same is hard, so very hard! I can only handle it if I know You are there with me. Are You with me?"

Silence.

"I say to God, my Rock, 'Why have You forgotten me? Why must I go about mourning, oppressed by the enemy?' My bones suffer mortal agony as my foes taunt me, saying to me all day long, 'Where is your God?'" (Ps. 42:9–10 NIV).

I cried out, "God, where are You? I can walk through anything if I can just feel Your presence, hear Your voice, and know You are here with me. Where are You, God?" The tears came—hot, tired, angry tears. "God, why have You gone silent?" There was so much more I wanted to say as I emptied my feelings to God that morning. "Life is difficult for so many people on this earth. Not only is it difficult to hear and obey You, sometimes it seems impossible." Like the psalmist David, "In my distress, I called upon the Lord, and He heard me and delivered me from all of my fears" (Rom. 34:4 KJV). I knew, if only by faith, God was hearing me in these trying moments, wherever He was. I needed Him to come to my rescue and deliver me from my strong enemy!

Except for a small lamp in a far corner, darkness and silence surrounded me and I felt like I was sealed in a tomb. I listened . . . listened to the nothingness. Then out of the stillness of the darkened corner of the room, I heard a familiar voice. It was as if it came from the burgundy tufted leather chair sitting by the small antique table where a lamp burned dimly. Just for a moment, in my thoughts, I wondered if He had been sitting there all the time, quietly observing me without speaking. But now, it didn't concern me. All that mattered was—*He's in my room and once again talking to me.*

The magnitude of His words still grip my heart, holding it together at all times. The One Who spoke was my closest companion, but I had never before heard the truth He spoke then. This voice was different today. The sound of the voice wasn't different, but what the voice said was strange. His words were, "Alan, it's not you who is being tried, but my words within you that are being tested."

From the depths of my innermost being, I questioned, "What did you say?"

The voice spoke again, "It's not you who is being tried, but my words within you that are being tested."

Although the voice seemed familiar, I paused and asked, "Is this You, God? Are You sure it's not me who is being tested?"

Why is my head spinning? Nausea, panic, and confusion overwhelmed me. *If it's not me being tested, then why is all of this happening inside of me?*

As I sat there, light began to shine through the dark shadows of my mind, birthing hope and assurance into the newness of life.

From deep within me, I trembled. In my mind I began to hear truths I didn't know. Was He revealing to me hidden secrets? I pondered this revelation and remembered the scripture, "Thy words have I hidden in my heart, that I might not sin against God" (Ps. 119:11 KJV). I began to realize the possibility of the greatest sin I could ever commit—not to believe in His words. This would be equal to not believing in God Himself.

The Word says, "In the beginning was the Word, and the Word was with God, and the Word was God" (John 1:1 NIV). These two are one; they are inseparable. It is impossible to believe in God and not believe in everything written by Him.

With these thoughts penetrating my mind and soul, I began to understand. If it was I alone being tested, I would completely fail. When health and finances cave in, humanity can be crushed, but by placing my confidence in God, the words He has spoken, the promises He has given, and the covenants He has made, it is impossible for me to fail! The clarity of this revelation drove fear out of my troubled spirit, enabling me not to take life's trials so personally.

Instead, it causes me to place all my trust in God. With renewed assurance, His sustaining power guarantees victory in every situation.

Ten days before, Barbara informed me we had to have $6,200 within two weeks. There was a downturn in the construction business, leaving us without any contracts or known income.

Reassuring, I reminded her, "God created the heavens and the earth and everything within, taking only six days. On the seventh day He rested. This means in just two weeks, He can create two heavens and two earths. I believe He will fulfill the miracle we need in the necessary time frame."

She nodded in agreement.

My confidence in God was settled deep within my heart. He would bring to us the miracle we desperately needed. Now, sitting in my study in the dark, it had been just ten days since Barbara and I had had this conversation.

Seven months earlier we had finished reconstruction on a home that had been heavily damaged with flood waters caused by a broken waterline. The repairs were complete and I submitted an invoice to the insurance company for the necessary restoration. After reviewing the documents, the homeowner refused to pay the remaining balance of $13,000. After three months of correspondence without results, I was convinced he would never pay me the remaining balance he owed.

At 7:20 on the morning of my encounter with God, where I had heard His reassuring words and felt the power of His holy presence, I knew without a doubt that we could conquer every foe. Regardless of any test that comes my way or problems life may throw at me, my confidence will remain, not in who I am, but in Who He is in me. His words, which are hidden in my heart, will cause me to become invincible! What I must do to receive God's protection and guidance through the difficult maze of life is to trust in the Lord with all my heart and lean not on my own understanding.

Barbara, smelling the aroma of fresh coffee, came down the stairs into the kitchen and saw biscuits rising in the oven. She couldn't believe I had breakfast already cooking. We sat down together at the table. With peace in my heart and a smile on my face, I told her of my early morning visitation with God and the revelation He had given to me. We were interrupted by the telephone ringing in the office.

The answering machine picked up, and the voice of a woman said, "I am calling to let you know my employer has written a check to you for moneys he owes your company."

She gave us the address of where we could pick up the check after 8:00 A.M. Barbara looked at me in amazement and said, "I wonder how much the check is for?"

Excited, I blurted, "It's a check—the amount is not important!"

Within minutes, I drove down Davis Boulevard to a nearby city, arrived at the corporate building, and walked into the receptionist's office. Greeting her, I introduced myself, and she politely handed me a sealed envelope with my name on it.

Chuckling with anticipation, I left the office, ripping the envelope open. My heart leaped within me when my eyes fell on the amount. It was $13,000, twice the amount we had to have to meet our needs and exactly the balance of what was owed. The faithful God had changed the heart of the man who said he would never pay!

After taking the check back to Barbara, I took a drive to enjoy the morning air, bubbling over with excitement. Coming to a stop sign, I saw a friend of mine, Ben Martin, whom I had not seen or talked to in a number of months. Gripping the steering wheel, I maneuvered across the street, while rolling down my window to greet him.

Smiling, Ben inquired, "Do you have time to talk awhile?"

Basking in joy, I assured him, "I do!" We parked our vehicles close by and I slid into his car.

In a serious tone, he haltingly began, "Alan, I just had a meeting with a wise counselor and friend. I desperately need an answer to something that is deeply troubling me. I'm reluctant to say this—it seems God has disappeared."

I could see the loneliness in his eyes. "Ben, what do you mean, He's disappeared?"

With difficulty, he continued, "It has been a long time since I have heard the voice of God. This morning I met with a trusted counselor, and probing his mind, asked, 'What's it going to take for God to speak to me again?'"

Immediately, with keen interest, I asked, "What did he say?"

"He struggled with his reply and really couldn't answer my question. I left his office without the answer, driving out of the parking lot with feelings of desperation grabbing at my heart. I was compelled to search for you, hoping I could find you and ask, 'Do you still hear His voice?'"

It wasn't coincidental that we stopped at the same stop sign, in the same city, at the same time. I knew it was an appointment God had made!

Those who know Ben know him as a man of integrity and honor. I consider it a privilege to do anything he would ask me to do, but I was not prepared for the questions he had for me. I was relieved that the first question Ben asked me wasn't difficult.

He asked, "Do you still hear from God?"

I was relieved. If he'd asked me this question a few days ago, I don't know how I would have answered. With exuberance, I replied, "Yes, I heard from Him this morning."

With hope saturating his countenance, Ben asked me a second question. "What do I need to do for God to speak to me again?"

Bewildered, I looked down, uncertain as to how I could answer something I didn't know and certainly couldn't control. I asked myself, *Why did God send this honest man to find me and ask a question that was impossible for me to answer?*

Slowly, I turned and looked at Ben, as the voice of the Holy Spirit instructed me, "Ask Him three questions." Intently, I obeyed the voice.

"Ben, how long has it been since God spoke to you?"

He glanced at me and said, "Two and one half years."

Clearing my throat and waiting for the next prompting, I asked, "Do you remember what God told you to do the last time He spoke to you?"

With mounting confidence, my friend replied, "I remember exactly what He told me."

Sitting quietly in deep meditation, it was rather awkward waiting for the final question. Finally, the voice continued, instructing me to ask him, "Did you do it?"

My heart sank as Ben confessed, "No. No, I didn't!"

Now I was speechless and didn't know what to say or how to respond. I remembered the struggles with my obedience to God, doing the difficult things. It's human nature to be this way. People do the best they can, yet there are times it seems impossible to do what God ask of us.

Then the loving voice of God spoke one more time within me, "Tell him to go and do it and I will speak to him once again."

With jubilation, I almost jumped out of my seat. I felt my heart leap within as I delivered the message God had just spoken to me. "Ben, go and do it, and He will speak to you again."

The meeting was over. Deep resolve was evident on his face, giving me confidence concerning the outcome—he would do whatever it was he should have done. I knew God would enable him to do it now!

Six weeks passed before I heard from him again. Early one morning, my telephone rang. It was Ben. I could hear the excitement in his voice. "Brother, can we meet for brunch?"

The sound of his voice activated my instant reply, "Absolutely, yes."

We agreed to meet at Cheddar's restaurant in a nearby city. Upon my arrival, Ben was sitting at a table waiting for me. He stood up and we greeted each other with an embrace, as only two men who respect each other can. We ordered our meal and as the waiter walked away, I asked him, "So, what's this all about?"

Joyfully, he began, "Early this morning, God spoke to me."

Chills went down my spine and I asked, "Did you do what God told you to do two and one half years ago?"

He looked at me with a sparkle in his eyes and said, "I did."

My heart was full as Ben and I left the restaurant that morning to go our separate ways. Both of our lives had been changed by the revelation of knowledge God had so graciously imparted to us. God's silence never means He has left us, nor does it mean He is angry. On the contrary, His silence causes us to trust with assured reliance on the character, ability, and strength of the mighty God, Who cannot and will not ever fail us. Obedience to God is far greater than any sacrifice or hardship we may encounter in our walk with Him.

> "As for God, His way is perfect; the word of the Lord is tried; He is a buckler to all them that trust in Him."
>
> —2 Samuel 22:31 KJV

CHAPTER 9

MAMA, THE EXORCIST

As long as I live, I will never forget that night! I was only seven years old, but today, even now, I can feel the pounding in my chest. I gasp for breath as I recall the dark and scary night with those five burning candles and the big wooden table, with my aunt leaning over it, waving her arms. I can see her as if it were all happening again right now! She had ripped off her clothes and all that remained was a full, white silk slip and a large, single strand of marble-like pearls around her neck, hanging down on her chest.

It all began at 11:30 P.M. on a Saturday night. My sister, brother, and I were sound asleep. In the darkness, I was jolted awake as my mother's hands shook me, whispering, "Get up. We have to go."

Jumping up, I was scared out of my wits. I reached for my cut-off blue jeans and grass-stained tennis shoes. I searched the floor frantically, wondering where they were. As my hand came in contact with my clothes, which somehow had slid under the edge of the bed, matters became even worse when I realized one of my tennis shoes was missing.

I thought, *No matter what, I have to hurry and find it.* I crawled on my stomach under the bed, where dust and spider webs hung from the bed springs and where the bogey man lives. But that night what I feared more than him was being left behind, alone in the dark. My skinny legs never ran faster! With one tennis shoe on and the other one in my right hand, I flew out the door and down the steps and dove into the back seat of the car, crashing into my brother's side.

In a flash, with gravel flying everywhere, my dad pulled out of the driveway and soon we were speeding toward downtown Ft. Worth. Finally, I gathered myself long enough to look up. Dark, empty streets were all I could see. When my dad turned right and headed south, I realized where we were going. This was the way to my Aunt Frieda's house. She was my mother's younger sister who was always in trouble. I scooted even closer to my brother as fear gripped me. I wondered, *What has she done now? What has happened? Has my aunt been killed? Or has she killed someone?*

As these thoughts went through my mind, my dad brought our car to a screeching stop in front of her house. I looked out the window and saw my uncle coming toward us in a big hurry to get to our car. He stuck his head inside my dad's rolled-down window and whispered, "Frieda's inside the house. She's been drinking all night long and taking pills—highballs."

I peeked over the seat. I had never seen a man as big as he was scared white before. He trembled and mumbled that Frieda was "calling on Satan to show himself by making the table walk."

That did it! Enough had been said! My daddy opened the car door and stepped out onto the curb, reached into his pocket, and pulled out a Camel cigarette. With his right hand he reached for his trusty, old chrome lighter I always wanted to play with. With one flick, it lit up like a torch.

In the flicker of the lighter I saw something I had never seen before. My dad's hands were shaking. After one big puff, he was ready to go. We all climbed out of the car and walked down the old, broken sidewalk, with my daddy leading the way.

Close behind him, with her head erect and her shoulders back, my ninety-eight-pound mother marched. In her right hand she firmly gripped her old, worn Bible. I can hear her, even now, as she spoke boldly in her heavenly language.

We entered the dark and spooky room and I could see five candles flickering from a small table. I could see the shadows of nine or ten men and women and a few children who cowered, crouched down against the walls. My sister, brother, and I quickly joined them, sitting down on the floor. Terrified, we stared at Aunt Frieda, who was twice the size of my mama.

She had already ripped off her clothes and flung them across the room. She stood at the end of the table, wearing only a slip that was stretched tight around her big body. She moved her arms from side to side and wore a large strand of white pearly beads around her neck. She moaned and groaned and cried. I covered my ears as she let out piercing screams. She demanded, through gritted teeth, for the devil to show himself and prove his presence by making the table walk.

In the dimly lit room, only three people stood. I kept one eye on the far corner, where I could see the glow of my daddy's cigarette. To the right of the table, I saw my mother standing with her treasured worn Bible in her hand. About five feet away, at the end of the table, my aunt Frieda stood. Everyone had their eyes on her as she began to scream and curse and order the table to walk.

The voice coming from her wasn't her voice. The snarling growls were not the sound of a woman, but of a great big, mean man! Everyone looked from her to the legs of the table as the voice coming out of her said, "Rise and walk!" Then she yelled again, "Rise and walk!"

All of a sudden, white balls flew throughout the room, glistening in the candlelight like balls of fire crashing into the screaming, terrified people who were sitting on the floor. They jumped up, screaming in full-blown panic, and emptied the room. They ran out the door, knocking each other down, slipping and sliding on those pearly white beads my aunt had ripped from her neck, slinging them all over the room. They fled in every direction into the darkness of the streets. My brother and I clung to each other, still sitting on the floor huddling behind our knees. I looked to the right side of the room, still seeing my dad standing there not moving.

I was terrified. I wanted to get up and run into the street, crawl beneath our old Studebaker car, and hide so no one could find me.

Then it happened! I heard the high-pitched, familiar voice of my ninety-eight-pound mama. She had already taken three quick steps and with her Bible in her right hand, she pushed it against Frieda's chest. With a voice mightier than the one that had come out of my aunt, she commanded, "In the name of Jesus, by the blood of the Lamb, devil come out of her!"

I was crouching low, looking underneath the table. I saw my Aunt Frieda crumble to the floor, weeping and crying. I will never forget what my mama did that night! She sat down close by her sister and placed Aunt Frieda's head in her lap, wiping away her tears and stroking her hair and face. She began to tell her how Jesus loved her and how He would make everything right.

Twenty minutes had passed since my mother had called the old devil out of my Aunt Frieda. Now, instead of tears of anguish, there were tears of joy streaming down her face as she joined my mama in singing her favorite song:

At the cross, at the cross, where I first saw the light,
And the burdens of my heart rolled away,
It was there by faith, that I received my sight,
And now I am happy all the day.

I sat there listening to my mother, my aunt, and even my dad singing the old hymn. The feeling of being scared was somewhat gone. "Happy all the day!" I thought, *I know what happiness is. That's running out of this room, down that old, broken sidewalk, and leaping into our old car and Dad driving away as fast as he can. That is what I call happiness!*

With these thoughts zooming through my mind, I looked over toward the dark corner and saw my sister, Sue, and brother, Dennis, whispering. I knew by the looks on their faces exactly what they were up to. Sure enough, the two of them had devised a plan to ensure we were going home before daybreak. They chose me to do something about it. This meant that I would have to go over to my mom, look up with my baby blue eyes, and tell her that I was sleepy and wanted to go home. It worked! I thought, *We are going home; we've escaped the dark cave where the old devil lived with the big wooden table I was certain I saw take a step with its legs!*

The next thing I remember is that my big brother and I slid down toward the middle of the bed and covered our heads, hiding so the bogey man would not find us while we were sleeping.

The months and years disappeared quickly, like snowflakes in an early winter Texas sun. Today I stand here looking at my reflection in a tall hallway mirror, reality staring back at me, portraying no longer a frightened little boy, enslaved by fear of the devil. Now I stand more than six feet tall and clothed in full battle gear, as my mama did all the days of her life. She taught me to stand firm in the time of battle against the spiritual forces of evil and sickness that attack us from the regions of the dark world.

Barbara and I have learned that we are not to fight life's battles alone. Therefore, we sent out an urgent appeal to men and women who were soldiers in Jehovah's army. Every one of them who received the summons came, wearing the full armor of God. All brought with them the shield of faith in one hand and in the other the sword of the Spirit, which is the Word of God. These mighty warriors, men and women of war, had learned to use their weapons skillfully and effectively in life's never-ending battles.

As I stood there in front of them, I was proud, yet humbled, and greatly honored to be counted among them. As I addressed them, their faces were filled with anticipation and their excited voices filled the room.

I saw Cullen Davis, his face handsomely chiseled with his chin set firm like flint. His eyes had pierced the darkness, seeking, searching, finding, and releasing those held in captivity by the evil one. There stood Ben Martin, erect and taller than anyone in the room. His face reflected an air of assurance and confidence in his God that is rarely seen.

By my side stood my faithful friend David Gregg, who had earned his name on the football field, "pit bulldog," but now he was on the battlefield for the lost, enslaved, and dying humanity. His aggressive nature displayed bravery that would stagger the enemy and cause him to retreat in defeat. To my left was Leonard Martin, so good, pure, and true. He was a man who could pray the sweetest prayer we thought would surely touch the heart of God.

Among this crowd of gallant warriors stood two handsome men whom I loved deeply. They are men of passion and students of God's Word, brothers Greg and Mark Wright. Shoulder to shoulder, we marched under the banner of Liberty Ministries, founded as our vehicle of war.

It enabled us to gain access into the chambers of those held in the darkness of fear and depression. Fearless, we entered into the catacombs of the occult, of warlocks and witches, liberating those held by drug addiction and alcohol dependency. Each and every one of them had been deceived by the cunning tactics of their mortal enemy, the devil, who had taken them captive. Through the avenues of television and radio, but greater than these, the voices of those set free from the bondage of slavery sent and brought loved ones to us from near and far.

I'm no longer a frightened little boy, crouching low, looking underneath the table. Now I am a warrior, dressed for battle, determined to take the fight to the front lines against the authorities, against the powers of this dark world and against the spiritual forces of evil in the heavenly realms.

I entered into the outer realms of the spirit world and domains I had not been aware of. The magnitude of their existence challenged my mind as I found myself astonished but not overwhelmed by their appearing.

Since the day of my encounter with the uninvited guest, a messenger angel sent from God, who requested I "ask God to reveal Himself" to me, my life, by supernatural means, changed

from darkness to light, making visible to all the striking altera-
tion in the character and the inward and outward man I was.
In the depths of my mind, never would I have comprehended
I would be translated into the celestial sphere where God and
His holy angels preside.

To be honored with a glimpse into the vastness of the mind
of the Creator, Whose thoughts are far above man's thoughts
as the heavens are above the earth, was unmerited. From there
I was carried down into the depths of hell—the domain of
Lucifer, the dragon, and his fallen angels, the demons.

I understand now that what I experienced as a child at the
hand of my mother in the living room in my aunt's house prepared me to become a representative of the kingdom of God
to make war against the old devil and his legions of darkness.
It is an old war formally declared by God in heaven when He
ordered Michael the archangel to evict the dragon and his angels from God's celestial dwelling place. Let's recall the initial
action that took place.

> "And there was war in heaven. Michael and his
> angels fought against the dragon, and the dragon
> and his angels fought back. But he was not strong
> enough, and they lost their place in heaven. The
> great dragon was hurled down—that ancient ser-
> pent called the devil, or Satan, who leads the whole
> world astray. He was hurled to the earth, and his
> angels with him."
>
> —Revelation 12:7–9 NIV

CHAPTER 10

PIERCING
THE DARKNESS

Slowly, I groped through the darkness of the large, fenced-in parking lot of a church in Euless, Texas. On that damp and creepy Halloween night, the smoke hung low in and around our heads—produced by twenty-five burning barrels filled with paraphernalia and pornographic materials and devices. Foul odors wafted from the belly of the incinerators.

More than five hundred victims, influenced by the devil, had responded to the challenge issued by means of radio blasts, inviting them to gather on the biggest night of the devil for the purpose of once and for all breaking loose from the chains of the evil one. Their anger saturated the very air we breathed as they celebrated with their loud, boisterous voices, yelling out vulgar insults toward one another. But more disgusting than their filthy language, which aroused my devil-confronting godly nature, were the blasphemous screams of profanity spitting out of their evil mouths, directed at the God of heaven, Who had made them.

As I pushed and shoved my way through the maddened mob, I caught a whiff of the intoxicating, smoldering self-rolled cigarettes peeking out of the puckered lips of one of the walking dead. Out of the darkness, broken only by the red-orange glow from the burning barrels, someone grabbed me by my right arm from behind. Abruptly, I jerked my head around, not knowing who or what had grabbed me.

Looking into the eyes of my interrupter, I saw a familiar face that momentarily softened my intensity. It was David Long, one of my many soldiers who walked with me. Still clutching my arm, he moved closer to me, whispering in my ear, "Pastor Alan, can you believe how many demoniacs there are here in this crowd of crazy people?"

A satisfied smile broke across my face as I replied, "David, I am more thrilled than I am surprised. This will be a night the angel of the Lord who keeps the Book will take his feathery quill dipped in blood and write down hundreds of names in God's Book of Life!"

Together he and I hurried through the wide open glass doors that gave everyone entrance into the auditorium of the church. Noisily, the crowd had dispensed of their burning cigarettes and cans of beer before they entered into the sanctuary, not knowing what was about to happen. The atmosphere changed dramatically as they came from the parking lot into the sanctuary and the band broke forth into joyful praise and holy worship to the one and only Lord God Almighty. When His presence fills a room, every knee in heaven and earth bows at the mention of His name. Now I was in my element; it was time to pierce the darkness!

Speaking freedom to those who were in captivity and declaring this as the night of the Lord, every demon had to flee. As I concluded the rousing message of forgiveness and liberation, all held as prisoners were asked to come forward with a challenge to leave their lives of the walking dead behind. They would be made whole by the cleansing of the blood of Jesus and liberated by the power of His resurrection.

I was amazed as more than two hundred lost and dying individuals pushed their way to the foot of the cross to make Jesus their Savior. There they found forgiveness through His mercies and grace. This was no longer a nomadic mob, for they had now enlisted into the army of the Lord!

Nothing is more rewarding than to walk into the regions of the damned, speaking the name of Jesus with His authority and releasing those held as prisoners. By then, the reputation of Liberty Ministries and the fateful Halloween night had been told near and far by radio, newspaper, and word of mouth. Our offices were inundated by phone calls, both local and from various parts of the nation. Their pleas for help did not go unanswered as we privately scheduled people of various ages, cultures, and locations to experience their opportunity for freedom.

Let me share two changed lives with you.

Jimmy

This engagement with the enemy involved the rescue and release of a nine-year-old boy we'll call Jimmy. He was an orphan in custody of the juvenile courts at the time. His birth mother had abandoned him in the front yard of distant relatives, and then she went on her way to live an immoral lifestyle. The results were devastating—producing an immensely damaged boy, seething with anger and desire for revenge because of the intense pain he had suffered. His outrage caused him to be removed from four foster homes. He had acted out—raining down terror with intent to cause great bodily harm to a female resident. Jimmy's saga repeated itself over and over.

Upon placement in each new foster home, his demeanor was that of a normal nine-year-old, complacent boy. Without warning, he slipped into uncontrollable psychopathic rages, his strength instantly that of a strong adult man. His voice changed from tenor tones to the deep, snarling, loud, and angry tones of a beast of a man. Everyone near him cowered in fear.

Each time he secretly secured a large butcher knife from the kitchen, targeting any females, young or old, in the immediate area. His hell-bent goal was to stab and kill them by plunging the knife into their backs. As I reviewed Jimmy's case, David Lovelace interrupted me by announcing his arrival with Jimmy.

A wide-eyed, blonde-haired, angry young man walked through my door. He crossed the threshold handcuffed to a large, burly woman who was an officer of a juvenile court. My assistant, a degreed counselor, instructed her to remove the restraints from his wrist and the shackles from his ankles and return to the lobby of the outer office to wait. David, in cooperation with the court-appointed psychoanalyst, who specializes in psychopathic behaviors, had arranged this meeting. Their attempts to administer healing with a variety of medical treatments had continually failed. Frustrated and befuddled, they turned to us. Our attempt was the last ditch effort to save this young lad.

At first I greeted him, "Hey, buddy, come give me a hug." I stooped down and extended my arms. He ran to me as if he were my long, lost son. When we met I grabbed him and stood up, hugging and swinging him from side to side. Then I carried him to the big leather sofa close by. He sat between me and David, my assistant, who placed a yellow writing pad and pencil into Jimmy's lap. With my arm around him, I asked him to draw me a picture of what made him feel happy. His face lit up with a big smile as he began to draw.

Seconds later, he proudly handed me his finished masterpiece. As I looked at it, I was quick to tell him how excellent the drawing was and one day he might become a great artist. His eyes beamed as he laid his head against my chest. With tears in his eyes, he said, "I love you." Reassuringly, I squeezed him and whispered back to him, "I love you, too."

I almost forgot about the picture! His drawing consisted of a zoo with a variety of animals in it. Instead of analyzing it, I asked him to show me around and tell me what he saw. His excitement accelerated as he pointed out the obvious to me— an elephant, a giraffe, a zebra, and of course, a monkey. Not fully comprehending the picture, I said, "Is this all?"

He turned his big brown eyes up at me, pointed at the picture, and said, "You don't get it!"

I looked closer and replied, "Get what?"

He smiled and said, "No bars."

Then I realized the animals were not in cages. They were free!

It took me a second to gather my composure, as I tried to hide the tears in my eyes. I asked him to draw one more picture. I instructed him, "Draw for me what it is that makes you sad and angry."

His demeanor quickly changed. He pulled away from me, his eyes narrowing and now icy cold. I felt a chill in the air, and I heard him grinding his clenched teeth as he drew his picture with vicious strokes. The more he expressed his hidden anger, the more I could hear the rumble rising from deep within his chest, like a volcano very close to eruption!

Intently, I kept one eye on him and the other on the yellow pad. The drama unfolded on his paper as he drew a stick person, which I interpreted to be an adult with a dress and long hair. She was repeatedly being stabbed in the back by a smaller stick person—a boy with a large knife with blood dripping from his hands! Then he began to stab the picture with the point of the pencil, again, again, and again, until he broke off the lead tip.

I had seen enough! I immediately grabbed both of his wrists and looked into his wild eyes. This is when I saw him! The serpent, the old devil, had bitten this young boy and with his fangs had injected his poisonous venom of unforgiveness into his heart. The poison caused excruciating pains of rejection that made him believe he was unwanted. It allowed hatred and murder to live through him. This assigned demon, in his deliberate, secret actions, had taken this innocent boy captive. The true origin of his sickness, shrewdly hidden from the observation of the skilled physicians who had treated him, was now exposed.

Immediately, I pulled the trigger and spoke the only name by which man can be saved. His is the only name the devil never wants to hear. "In the name of Jesus, upon His authority, I command every demon of hatred, murder, and unforgiveness to loose him and let him go!"

A momentary struggle took place as the strength of a powerful being emerged. The deep, snarling, angry voice spoke no more. It had been silenced. The young boy fell over into my arms with tears running down his cheeks and a smile on his face. "Rescue" was complete when he asked Jesus into his heart. "Release" had to be executed with this directive—he must forgive his mother and all others who had hurt him!

Without reluctance, Jimmy whispered, "Mama, I forgive you. I will always be sad, but I'm not mad at you anymore."

He followed instructions easily, and after a short time he walked out into the lobby with my arm around his neck to meet the lady officer. When he saw her, he ran to her with his arms outstretched and his eyes full of joy and grabbed her around the waist. The officer looked at me in astonishment with the chains of his bondage still in her hands. She said, "It seems I will not need these anymore!"

The same physicians who once had no answer for him declared Jimmy safe and sound less than thirty days later. He was released into a wonderful foster home. When I inquired about him some seven months later, the report was, "All is well." This wonderful young man was free at last, living free in a world without bars!

Gadara

The drizzly winter clouds hung heavy over the big, fenced-in parking lot. As I stood there staring out the large plate glass windows, I could see in the distance flashing lights of emergency vehicles trying to weave their way through the stalled traffic on the freeway. The sounds of blaring fire truck horns blended with the unmistakable shrill sirens of police cars and ambulances, notifying us that somewhere close by tragedy had struck without warning.

As I stood there captivated by thoughts of how fragile life can be, here today and gone tomorrow, my thoughts were interrupted by the penetrating smell of the rich aroma of fresh coffee. Turning back toward the open door of my office, I was greeted by David, my assistant, with a steaming cup of coffee. In his left hand was a pink telephone message sticky note.

He began awkwardly, "Good, hot fresh coffee first or the bad news? Which will it be?"

Looking intently at his face, I quizzingly replied, "Which one should I take first, the coffee or the phone call?"

He stood there with his big eyes twitching and his lips beginning to tremble as he spoke through broken sounds, revealing that something was desperately wrong. "I think it should be the coffee first."

I took a deep breath and whispered, "Give me both!" Sliding my calloused fingers into the handle of the green coffee cup and gripping it securely in my left hand, I took a long sip of its rich flavor, trying to read the troubled expression on the face of David. I reached quickly and took the pink telephone message card from his hands.

Unable to restrain myself, I quickly looked at the name of the caller. Written on the paper in large black letters was the name Deborah Hollingsworth, Phoenix, Arizona, a name I did not know. I relaxed, asking him if he talked personally to the caller. Out of his big brown eyes, tears begin to spill down his face.

Stumbling, he began, "This is the worst case I have ever heard of!"

Looking at him in stunned amazement, I returned to my desk, laying the pink telephone message on my big black desk, leaning back, taking a sip of my now lukewarm coffee. My mind quickly surveyed many of the past faces David and I had encountered in the ministry of exorcism. Flashing before my eyes, I saw saddened, dejected faces of suicidal men and women trapped previously in the death grip of hopelessness and despair; the darting, suspicious eyes of more than a dozen lesbian girls from a university in a nearby city, whose lives had been victimized by evil predators; and witches and warlocks, wearing black and white makeup, emphasizing their hard, cold eyes that were full of hatred. The unloved, despised humanity of all ages were black, white, yellow, or brown—no one had escaped the tortuous terror at the hand of the abusing demonic accuser. We had ministered to all of these without fear or apprehension.

In shocked disbelief I looked at David and asked, "How could this be the worst we have ever encountered?" David's face flushed and his eyes bulged as he pointed his shaking finger at the pink telephone message card and said, "This woman's sister has mutilated herself!"

He turned abruptly without excusing himself and left my office in grievous exasperation. There was no mistaking his reaction. David wanted us to storm the prison walls of self-hatred with the battering ram of the Word of God until they crumble under our feet, giving us access to set the captive free.

As I heard the door of his office close behind him, I reached across my desk for the telephone and, without further reluctance, dialed Phoenix, Arizona. Five rings later the phone was answered by a woman. "Hello."

I said, "This is Alan Youngblood. Is this Deborah?"

She answered, "Yes, it is."

Politely, I said, "I'm returning your phone call this morning to Liberty Ministries. How is it we may be of help to you?" I sat there waiting for a reply, but all I heard was silence. "Deborah, are you still there?" I inquired.

I heard sobs, and then with a whispering voice she said, "Jesus, help me. My sister is demon-possessed!"

Momentarily, I was caught off guard by this initial phraseology Deborah chose. Composing myself, I inquired, "How did you arrive at this conclusion?"

She made no immediate reply and I heard nothing but silence. I prompted her, "Deborah, I am not being skeptical, but it is very important to me to know why you would say your sister is demon-possessed. Please explain this to me or I cannot help you."

I heard more sniffling and crying. I pressed her to talk to me by speaking directly about oppression and possession, reminding her of the difference. "Oppression is a person who is crushed with a heavy burden that is more than they can bear. It severely affects them spiritually and mentally. Now, Deb, remember that possession is when the normal personality is replaced by another, this being an evil spirit that controls or dominates its victim's actions to carry out dastardly deeds. It is extremely important for you to convince me which one you believe your sister is held in."

She tried again. "My sister, Gadara, is thirty years old; she lives alone. For fifteen years she has been a hostage, joining in with the hordes of darkness led by the devil on a brutal onslaught against her own body." More sobs. "The first time she tried to kill herself was three years ago, when she took a sharp knife, severing her wrist with fatal intentions.

"She lay there, alone in her mobile home, and someone summoned the medics with an emergency call to 9-1-1. She was rushed to the hospital, dying from the volume of blood she had lost. They gave her transfusions to save her life."

"Well, is she okay now?" I inquired.

"No, it's worse than ever. The evil influence in her mind has induced her to commit the crime of sadistic alterations against her own self!" she blurted.

"Are you speaking of suicide?" I asked.

"Pastor Alan, what I'm saying is . . . more than twenty times she has attacked her own body. The latest was the most brutal of all."

"What is her condition right now?"

Anxiously, she replied, "She called me a few months ago, telling me she hated herself and her ugly face. Her last words to me were, 'I'm going to make myself pretty.' She walked down to the hardware store and took what little money she had and bought a hacksaw and used it as a scalpel to saw her nose off of her face. She liked the results, moving to her ears and sawing them off also."

I could hear hysteria rising in Deborah's voice as she continued, "If this was not enough, she stuck her tongue out in front of the mirror and sawed it in half!"

Unable to hide my shock, I blurted, "Deborah, stop it. Enough! I need you to calm down. I'm going to help you and Gadara."

I tried to conceal the explosions I was feeling inside of me of hatred and anger toward the despicable devil. Taking a deep breath, I carefully directed her to bring her sister, Gadara, to me as soon as possible. "Don't allow anything or anyone to stop you from bringing her to us. I promise we can help your sister!"

Relieved, she answered, "Okay, I don't know how with words to say thank you, but your ministry is our last hope."

"We're excited that you have given us this opportunity to be a part of Gadara's healing. We are looking forward to meeting you and your sister soon." With those final words, I transferred her to David to arrange the appointment and schedule the meeting. Ten minutes passed before I heard David knocking at my office door. Looking up from my scribbling of the notes I had written concerning Gadara and her terrible situation, I raised my voice and said, "David, come in."

Breathing a sigh of relief, he asked, "Where do we go from here?"

"I'm not sure," I told him.

He took another deep breath and calmly said, "I know what I'm going to do. Fast. For the next seven days, I'm going to drink liquids only, read the Word of God, and get ready."

I looked at him calmly and said, "There's only one thing I'm certain of. When Gadara arrives, so will our God with all of His glory filling the room, and His power will bring down every demon that possesses her."

David rose slowly to his feet, nodding his head in agreement as he returned to his office to meditate on God's Word.

Seven days went by as swiftly as tumbleweeds flying through the air in the howling winds on a West Texas plain. Today would be Gadara's deliverance day, the day that would always be remembered as her moment of liberation. I sat there at my desk with my Bible opened to the Gospels that relate to the story of one called Legion, whom Christ rescued from the dark caverns of the damned. In my studies as I prepared for this battle, I meditated upon the definition of war. It is most often defined as an open, declared, armed conflict between states or nations. It's comprised of soldiers armed and equipped for battle.

At this moment, the voice of the Holy Spirit quickened me to turn to the pages St. Paul penned while a prisoner in Rome. His inspirational writings challenge us to take on a radical new identity.

"Finally, be strong in the Lord and His mighty power. Put on the full armor of God, so that you can take your stand against the devil's schemes. For our struggle is not against flesh and blood, but against the rulers, against the authorities, against the powers of this dark world and against the spiritual forces of evil in the heavenly realm" (Eph. 6:10–12 NIV).

In conflicts of this nature, it is vital that we be clothed with the armor of God and equipped with the knowledge of the Word, enabling us to brandish skillfully the sword of the Spirit and prepare to fight in soul-strewn trenches, at all times expecting aerial support from on high.

Then we will take down the kingdoms of this dark world, of drugs, alcohol, and immorality, causing sickness and every manner of disease to bow its knee, proclaiming the exploits of the mighty God and His army.

These battlegrounds are located in the hearts and minds of people. Being fully convinced, we were ready for the adventure to begin. Together we waited for Gadara to arrive. One could cut the tension with a knife as David and I sat motionless with breathless anticipation. We were certain Christ Himself would show up on the scene and save the day!

At last, the doorbell rang from the small waiting room nearby. David's eyes widened from either fear or anticipation as he walked toward the outer lobby to meet and escort Gadara and her sister for their long-awaited appointment.

Within minutes the door to the inner office swung open with David leading the way. He stood looking at me like a deer in headlights, ready to bolt and run. My eyes shifted from him to the side of the room where she stood. It was the most grotesque sight, and the odor coming from her tried, with all its might, to suffocate me. I was aware it was not hers alone but the presence of thousands of unclean spirits who inhabited her very being.

I thought I was prepared, but as I looked at her face, her atrocious appearance really shocked me. She didn't have a nose, just two small holes leading directly into the facial cavity. I noticed her ears were really gone. Her greasy black hair lay flat against her head with streaks of dirty gray mingled through it.

She brought her hand up to her mouth, as if timid or embarrassed because I was staring at her so intently. Then I noticed two fingers missing on one hand and possibly three missing on the other—more mutilation. Her appearance and the odor repulsed me to such a degree that I turned to walk away, not wanting to look at her or smell her any longer.

And as I turned, I heard an audible voice—the voice of Christ speak to me, "Alan, meet Miss Demoniac!" I froze in my tracks and in my mind I went back two thousand years to when Christ Himself chose to go to the region of Gerasenes. In the Bible, the story reads like this:

> When Jesus got out of the boat, a man with an evil spirit came from the tombs to meet him. This man lived in the tombs and no one could bind him any more, not even with a chain, for he had often been chained hand and foot, but he tore the chains apart and broke the irons on his feet. No one was strong enough to subdue him, night and day. Among the tombs and in the hills, he would cry out and cut himself with stones.
>
> —Mark 5:2–5 NIV

After recalling the story in my mind, I turned toward her with tears in my eyes. Never before that day or since has God honored me to such an extent, placing me in that moment into Jesus' sandals where He stood 2,000 years before, with the greatest opportunity—to be as He was and to do what He did. This was the greatest pleasure that He and I had shared so far on our journey together!

I instantly abandoned all my strategy for warfare as God's Holy Spirit whispered in my ear what to do. I walked up to

her with my arms opened wide. Looking past the ugliness of
her face and fighting to keep the odor from repelling me, I
wrapped my arms around her and held her as if she were my
long, lost sister. I whispered in the small hole where an ear had
previously been, "I love you."

With the nubs of her hands where fingers had once been, she
pushed me slowly away from her, looked at me with eyes of
amazement, and spoke. Her words were difficult to understand
because she had sawed off a section of her tongue. She asked,
"Wha- did ou- jus- sa?"

I repeated my statement to her, "I love you." She had a bewildered look on her face so I asked, "Did you not understand
what I said?"

"Oh, I unerstood ou the firs ime! I jus wantd to ear it agin."

We were on our way to our new strategy of warfare that
completely confused our enemy. He thought we would make
a frontal attack, and honestly, that is what I'd prepared for, but
my warring partner, the Holy Spirit, was directing this battle.
He spoke to me, "Be as wise as the serpent but as harmless as
the dove." This secret strategy would bring complete victory
into the life of an innocent victim who had been held hostage
for all these years.

Not to deceive you and yet not to reveal the essence of the
battle, there was warfare, and the old devil and his hordes of
darkness were driven out. Her body became a temple of the
Holy Spirit, where He would now dwell and darkness would
rule in her no more! I still see her smiling face today, as if it was
only yesterday. As they walked away from me toward the open
door, she stopped, pulled away, and ran back to me with her
arms flung open wide. Gadara grabbed me with a big bear hug
and whispered in my ear, "I uve ou!"

She turned and left like a school girl who had found her true love; and she had. His name is Jesus.

Solemnly, I walked slowly over to the plate glass window overlooking the big fenced parking lot and watched the jubilant sisters enter their car and drive away. I stood there with mixed emotions. Certainly there was joy because a new name had been written in the Lamb's Book of Life. Personally, I could not take any credit for what had occurred with Gadara; I had almost turned my back and walked away. Had it not been for the "voice" of Christ speaking to me and pouring His compassion into my innermost being, I would have failed to do my part for the kingdom of God and lost humanity.

Tears coursed down my face as I remembered Calvary, where the Lamb of God suffered an excruciating beating as He staggered up the rocky road on the Via Dolorosa, wearing a crown of thorns on His precious head. Finally he reached the top of the hill called Golgotha, where the Romans drove large spikes into His hands and feet, nailing Him to a cruel cross. There He suffered, bled, and died for the sins of one like Gadara, me, and you!

I shudder to think of what would have happened if He had turned His back on all of us, who are sinners, and walked away from the cross, leaving us lost and dying in the darkness . . . But— He—didn't! And neither do you have to walk away. Together, you and I can kneel at the foot of His cross and ask Him to forgive us of all of our sins.

I hope you'll pray this prayer with me now: "Father, God, I am a sinner, lost and dying in the darkness. I desperately need your Son, Jesus, to save me. I ask You in His name to forgive me of all the sins I have committed. Wash me, cleanse me, and change me into a brand new person and write my name into the Book of Life. Amen!"

It wasn't so difficult, was it? Of course not, for He has already done the hard part. All we have to do is confess our sins and believe in our hearts that we are forgiven and then we will be saved. Now all you have to do is rejoice and follow Him! "For God so loved the world He gave His one and only Son, that whoever believes in Him, shall not perish, but have eternal life" (John 3:16 NIV).

Warning!

The author suggests no one attempts exorcisms without prior experience in this field. See Acts 19:13–16. Only in this chapter have the names of Jimmy, Gadara, and Deborah been changed to protect their identities.

CHAPTER 11

PUT MY WORDS
IN HER

I heard my daddy yell from our screened in back porch. "Alan Dee, it's time to eat!" His big strong voice interrupted the sand lot football game I was playing with five of my buddies in our backyard.

I hollered back, "Just five more minutes, Daddy." These five minutes became ten or fifteen until finally I was able to break away from the last defender and sprint to the goal line—the one we scratched in the dirt with a stick. I threw the old pigskin football as high into the air as I could, yelling, "Touchdown, we win!"

With my heart pumping with the thrill of winning, I turned and ran toward the back porch, celebrating all the way. With one big leap, I was on the porch and opened the screen door that slammed behind me. I yelled, "I'm home, Dad!"

My only thought entering the kitchen was, *I'm starving.* On the side burner of our old cook stove, I spied my favorite food Dad had cooked for supper—fried bologna sandwiches with mustard and fried potatoes with onions. Mama wasn't home that night.

Mama was a nurse at Harris Hospital downtown Ft. Worth, so Daddy served as chief cook. In the background I remember big, bellowing sounds of laughter coming from my daddy in our living room. Our favorite television show was already under way.

Not wanting to miss even one more minute, I grabbed my food and placed it on a TV tray, ran into the living room, and sat down quickly on the sofa to lock my eyes on our seventeen-inch black-and-white television set.

He was the funniest man alive, Jerry Lewis, our favorite comedian. I can still see Dad with his old tattered white handkerchief in his hand, laughing, crying, and blowing his nose as we savored every minute of *The Dean Martin and Jerry Lewis Show*. We both loved and enjoyed Jerry, a natural-born comedian who brought happiness to thousands of people.

It is true, time does fly. On Labor Day 1986, I found myself alone in my upstairs sitting room still watching Jerry Lewis. But this time I watched on a large-screen television set, and Jerry was no longer a comedian. Instead, this beautiful, sensitive man had grown into a giant crusader, fighting for the very lives of tens of thousands of precious people victimized by the dreadful disease of muscular dystrophy.

While I sat there with tears in my eyes and a smile on my face, into my room walked my beautiful sixteen-year-old, middle daughter, Tamara. When I looked up at her, I saw a courageous, loving person with tears twinkling out of the corners of her big, brown, pear-shaped eyes. She looked down at me. Her request was clear and understood—

"Are we going to do our part and send a pledge to Jerry to help him in finding a cure for this debilitating disease?" Her words had hardly left her lips when I reached for my billfold and took out my American Express credit card.

I handed it to her and said, "You make the call and give what you decide."

I watched her leave the room and my conscience was shredded. I realized this was the first time I had ever contributed to this great cause, even though I had watched Jerry on Labor Day many times through the years.

The journey that would carry us from spectator to participator for Jerry's cause started the year before, in Washington, D.C. on a summer day in June of 1985. The Youngbloods were on vacation—all of us—Alan and Barbara, Taleesa, Tamara, and Tricia—with our closet friends. David and Linda Gregg and their three daughters were high-stepping up the many flights of steps leading to the Lincoln Memorial. Halfway up, I stopped to grab a breath of fresh air. Out of habit, I turned to do a head count, scanning down the massive steps, looking for familiar faces in the crowd.

My heart skipped a beat when I counted only nine—there should be ten heads. One was missing! Every muscle in my body tensed and I looked frantically from face to face, searching for the one who was missing. Finally, in the midst of the crowd of people, only three steps from the bottom, I saw her! Tamara was bent over, holding her knees with both hands, as if she was struggling not to fall. A few steps below me I saw my wife, Barbara, with an expression on her face I recognized that said, *Get to her, quick!*

Instantly, I bounded down the steps three to five at a time, dodging through the masses as they ascended. Finally, I reached her with my chest pounding from the anxiety in my heart. My first words exploded out of my mouth, "Sweetheart, what's wrong?"

Before leaving Texas, our three daughters had attended cheerleading camp in preparation for the coming fall semester. All three had been or were cheerleaders at Christian Temple School where they attended. Taleesa, who had just graduated a few months earlier, attended camp as an assistant instructor. Tamara and Tricia had just concluded the five days of cheerleading boot camp only three days prior to our family vacation in Washington, D.C. Tamara's eyes were on me, and I saw the worried expression on her face. It was much more than just being out of breath. She spoke painfully, "Daddy, I don't know. I can't lift my legs to take another step."

This was extreme for Tamara and totally out of character for her. I lifted her onto my back and—with her arms wrapped around my neck—we headed up to the top to catch up with all the rest who were waiting for us. As we reached the top where Barbara was still waiting, she said, "What's wrong?"

Gasping for air, I could hardly answer her. As Tamara slid down to the landing below, I said between breaths, "Now's not the time for this discussion because none of us knows the answer." All the others hurried on from the Lincoln Memorial to the Washington Monument. Barbara, Tamara, and I walked slowly, holding hands, stopping frequently to rest and asking Tamara what she was experiencing.

She said, "Every muscle in my body is sore. To walk or use my arms is just misery." She continued to describe her symptoms, and it became crystal clear to me what the diagnosis had to be.

I became more and more relieved as I explained to her exactly what I thought was going on in her body. After all, as an athlete, I had been in her situation many times after rigorous workouts in football practice and games. So the solution was quite simple to me. The cheerleading camp was probably the culprit. The strenuous exercises she had gone through had brought on her body discomfort. The cure would take one or two days of liniment applications and muscle massage and in no time, Dad would have her as good as new.

The next morning, I was certain her improvement would be near miraculous, but I was wrong. I watched her strain to place one foot in front of the other as we attempted to continue seeing various sights and museums in the capital city. The pain of watching her in misery, attempting to keep up, became too much, so Barbara decided to return to the hotel with Tamara. They remained there for the next two days of our vacation.

Tamara's condition continued to deteriorate for the next three weeks. Shockingly, our family physician became more and more uncertain of a diagnosis. He recommended we take her to a neurologist, who specialized in muscle diseases. His concerned phone call to the specialist allowed us to get an appointment the following day. When we arrived at the doctor's building, I felt confident that this highly skilled specialist would immediately know what the answer was and alleviate the muscle weakness expediently. After all, this fine team of physicians was supposed to be the best in the Southwest.

From the beginning, they were personal and communicative. Their thorough examinations, including blood tests, didn't bring the quick solution we had hoped for. Instead, it started us down a path that seemed to lead to destruction and death. They feared Tamara had a rare strain of muscular dystrophy and if so, the quality of life she had always enjoyed before would never again be a reality for her.

Barbara and I appreciated the quick actions of this team of specialists. Within three days, we checked Tamara into Harris Hospital to have a biopsy on the muscle of her right leg, which we hoped would give the doctors the possible answer we so desperately needed.

Surgery came shortly after the crack of dawn. I personally struggled with drinking coffee and eating a donut that morning because Tamara was not allowed to eat after midnight. How could I enjoy food if my daughter could not? We waited for more than an hour and a half for her turn in surgery. I looked at her parched lips and asked her if she would like some water, or better still—a cup of ice with a little bit of Sprite. She took a small sip of it before the nurses and anesthesiologists arrived.

Barbara and I walked down the hall to the double doors of the surgery room and both kissed her good-bye and told her we loved her. Little did we realize at this time that this could be our final good-bye to our darling daughter. As the double doors closed behind us, we sadly went to the closest waiting room to wait for the one-hour procedure.

Within fifteen minutes, we heard an emergency call, though it was in a code name we were not familiar with. Two technicians arrived with a machine and entered hurriedly into the surgery room where our daughter was. Our hearts fell deep into the pit of our stomachs and our breath became extremely laborious as we sensed there was a struggle of life and death going on. I couldn't stand it any longer! I went through the double doors and before someone stopped me, I saw the surgical team working feverishly over my daughter. I knew immediately she was fighting for her life.

I had no choice but to return to the waiting room. I was shaking, and I called upon God to spare her life. Barbara and I sat there without speaking for a long time. There were just no words. When the operating physician entered the room, his face was full of anger. Through gritted teeth he demanded, "Which one of you gave Tamara food prior to surgery?"

"No one!" I shouted. "She hasn't had anything but a small sip of Sprite in the last ten hours." I was becoming angry, too. I said, "Forget the food and tell me my daughter's condition!"

He began to tell us that shortly after the anesthesiologist's procedure, Tamara had begun to aspirate. The fight to keep vomit out of her lungs became a life-and-death struggle that went on for more than fifteen minutes. She had really stood at death's door. The doctor vowed, "I will get to the bottom of this and find out what went wrong. If it wasn't food, then she must have had a reaction from the anesthesia."

We breathed a sigh of relief as we stood by our precious daughter in the recovery room. Thankfully, we checked her out later the same day, knowing death had tried to steal her from us.

Five days later, we returned to the doctor's office to learn the results of the muscle biopsy. We were confident the news would be good. After all, Tamara had always been a perfectly healthy child. Why and how could anything like this touch one of my daughters?

Then the news we had waited for came as one of the elite team of specialists entered the room and described the results of the biopsy. His words hit Barbara and me like a bomb. He looked at the three of us with eyes of concern and spoke softly, telling us the lab tests had revealed that this dreaded disease had entered Tamara's nervous system and had already begun its deadly assault. He continued, "The effects are irreversible. The severing of the nerves is clearly identifiable but further tests will be necessary to determine the full extent of this fatal disease that has attacked your daughter."

The shock of the diagnosis exploded in our ears! These sobering thoughts—that our fifteen-year-old daughter was already and would continue to become an invalid and a prisoner in her own body, from which there was no escape except by an agonizing death, were more than we could bear! The unrelenting assault on our precious daughter continued as we watched her deteriorate before our eyes, rendering her all but helpless within a five-month rampage. This team of specialists was somewhat stunned at the speed of this killer that raged inside her body, causing concern about how long she might live. They estimated that most likely she would live less than one year.

The days became more and more difficult and the nights all but impossible for us to face, as Tamara's soreness from the muscle inflammation soared to unheard of heights in a very short time. We watched her reach a place where she could not sit up in bed on her own or stand up without help. She walked, scooting her feet a half step at a time, very slowly. Her arms were drawn and hardly usable, filled with dozens of small, marble-like substances. Her throat, we were told, would be the last place of the attack, rendering it difficult for her to swallow solid foods without choking.

She needed help to comb her hair, take a bath, or handle all the normal necessities of a fifteen-year-old girl's daily care. She found it utterly impossible to get up from the bed!

She was bowed but not beaten, with an entourage of dedicated high school friends surrounding her. Tamara, determined, continued her studies. Undaunted, she trudged on, dragging one foot after the other. When she was no longer able to carry her own books with her crippled, drawn arms, close friends like Julie Mullins came to her aid, carrying her books in one arm and Tamara's in the other.

Systemically and continually, the crippling disease took its toll on her fragile body. Three steps up a flight of stairs, she was unable to take even one more step. But who needed legs with a cousin like Delania Utter, who saw her fall to her knees, clutching the hand rail precariously with her crippled arms, holding on desperately and unable to regain her footing. Kneeling there on the steps, embarrassed at her dilemma, Tamara heard a familiar voice. Turning, she looked up into the face of her cousin Delania, who had laid her books down, ready to hoist Tamara on her back.

Eagerly, she said, "I'll carry you up the stairs."

Tamara smiled, still trying to be independent. "I can make it if you will help me. These stairs are so steep there's no way I can climb them by myself."

Her loving cousin reached down, sliding her strong arms under Tamara's. Stabilized, the two began the long trek slowly, one painful step at a time. Halfway up, the tardy bell rang. They looked at each other. Tamara, biting her lower lip, said, "You go on up to class. I'll get there as soon as I can."

Undaunted, Delania replied, "No! I'm going to walk with you all the way!"

As they entered the classroom, she helped Tamara to her desk. Satisfied, she turned to hurry to her class, late but happy. I don't know if their classmates applauded the two brave cousins, but I am certain all of heaven gave them a standing ovation.

Barbara was devastated at the thought that we could be burying our daughter. Hope began to perish. Depression began to make its home in Barbara's heart. When I came in from work, I found her in the bedroom or locked behind closed doors, hoping to escape the inevitable. She walked around in a daze, not able to do the chores that had always been so easy for her.

As for me, I was frustrated beyond imagination. Being a husband and father who had always protected his family from any thing or person who intruded uninvited into our lives, I began to search within myself for the door I had possibly left open to allow this vicious enemy access into my home to attack my daughter. *Where and how did he invade our lives? Was it my fault, had I failed in some way? What in the world had I done that would leave my daughter unprotected, causing her to become a victim of this muscle disease?*

I called on God to search my life and show me where I had fallen short as a man of God, a husband, or a father, and whatever it was, I would ask God to forgive me and hold me responsible—not my daughter. I requested, without relenting, "God, take this disease off of my daughter and place it on me!" The more I prayed, the more frightened and desperate I became. Peace? I looked for it, but I couldn't find it. Hope escaped my grasp. Despair began to settle over me like darkness, leaving me groping as a blind man.

During this time, my construction company was building five homes, including our personal home. Every one of them was scheduled for completion by the end of the fiscal year. The difficulties and the demands of our clients to meet this deadline were unending. Not one of them knew we were caught in the jaws of a vicious killer who had entered into our lives uninvited, unannounced, and unwanted in its plans to destroy our happiness and our dreams.

Late one evening I stood on the second-floor balcony of the room that was to be Tamara's room in our new home. The paint colors, the wallpaper, and the carpet, all a combination of peach and green, had been selected by Tamara from samples brought to her by her mother. As I looked into her room, tears flooded my eyes. I didn't know if she would ever see, much less occupy, her bedroom. I screamed at the top of my voice, "God, if my daughter dies and cannot live here in this house, then neither will I, nor any of my family. We will walk away and never occupy this place!"

Each day seemed like a living hell. If screaming, throwing up, or slamming my head against the wall would have solved my problem, I would have done it with a vengeance, but I realized I could do nothing, and neither could this wonderful medical team who had searched endlessly for answers to save my daughter.

I had reached the end of myself. I talked to God night and day. I know my voice was heard in His temple and in His ears continually. All of heaven became familiar with the sound of my voice and the cry of my petition. I cried out from the depths of everything within me. I pleaded to the one and only God, Who could heal my daughter and spare her life—not because of who we are, but because of Who He is.

The end of the matter loomed closer than I realized. One Wednesday night, out of duty alone, Taleesa, Tricia, and I attended the mid-week church service. Even the desire to go to church escaped me. Like robots, we walked in and carried out our duties. Mine was to teach a Bible class, and the girls attended a youth group called Rock church. We drove home without conversation because of the devastating news given to us earlier in the day: a blood test had revealed Tamara's muscle inflammation had reached 2130 points and we were told the average person who is without muscle soreness is 225 points. They gave the example of an NFL football player who carried the ball thirty times in one game and whose muscle inflammation likely would not exceed 380 points. The average person, through strenuous activity, probably could not raise theirs to more than 300 points, and this is the basis for muscle soreness.

We were instructed that the following Tuesday they would do a final test to document and enter into her file final proof of muscular dystrophy.

This would be entered and submitted to the beloved Jerry Lewis Foundation that gallantly helps raise funds to find a cure for this dreadful disease. Tamara was uninsured, so the thousands of dollars we had spent would be documented, applied for, and possibly reimbursed at a later time.

With death stinking up the air we breathed every day, we arrived home at 9:30 P.M. Barbara fitfully tossed in bed. I went into Tamara's room, where a small night light shined a glow bright enough that I could see her closed eyes. Tears flowed freely down my cheeks and one last time I pleaded, "God, don't let my daughter die. Spare her! Raise her up as a living testimony of Your power and Your grace." As I cried out my last and final plea, I kissed her on the cheek. And when my tears touched her face, she looked up at me and managed a smile. I whispered, "I love you, sweetheart."

I slipped into bed, trying not to wake my wife. The lamp on the nightstand was on and the Bible was lying on her chest, still open. I lifted it from her and began to flip through the pages aimlessly, hoping somewhere I might read something that would bring a ray of hope to me. Nothing I read said anything that made sense that night. I closed the book, feeling alone and dejected.

As I reached to turn out the lamp, an audible voice spoke to me and said, "Put my words in her and I will heal her." Jolted, I sat up and looked around the room. I saw no one, but I could sense the presence of the mighty God.

I quickly turned to the concordance, thinking I had read something similar to this before. I searched frantically and there it was: Psalm 107:19–20, "Then they cried to the Lord, in their trouble, and He saved them from their distress. He sent forth His Word and healed them, He rescued them from the grave" (NIV).

My heart leaped. I shook Barbara awake and told her God had just spoken to me. Half asleep, she murmured, "What did He say?"

He said, "Put my words in her and I will heal her."

As she turned over, she mumbled, "What could this mean?"

I didn't offer her a response. The meaning of the words from the voice that had spoken was not clear to me—not yet.

All three of my daughters were raised in church. They were taught the Word of God all of their lives. So somehow I had to get understanding because if I obeyed the voice, I knew Tamara would be healed.

The following day, I talked to God for hours, asking—inquiring—what He had meant by His instruction, "Put my words in her and I will heal her."

Then I heard His voice again. "It is the simple things that will confound the wise." I had the answer I desperately needed. I knew what I had to do.

Immediately after dinner the next evening, I called my family together. Taleesa and Tricia sat to my left with one empty chair beside me. Barbara sat next to me on my right. We all waited for Tamara, who refused to let anyone assist her to the room. We heard the *swish, swash, swish*, as she scooted her feet across the floor, dressed in her nightgown and soft slippers. She painfully and slowly inched her way to the chair, where I stood up and lifted her into the seat. Just being touched brought great pain to her body which was ravaged by this deadly disease.

I looked around at my three daughters, and I asked them, "Do you recall through the years on many occasions I have told you God has spoken to me? I always related to you what He said. Do you remember, each time, at a later time all of these words happened just as God said?"

All three chimed in together, "Yes."

I recounted to them what God had said to me the night before and today when He said, "It is the simple things that will confound the wise."

I said, "Tonight I am going to read a story that you are familiar with from Sunday school."

They nodded their heads in agreement.

It was nothing profound, and I knew it wouldn't be a new revelation. It was the story of the three Hebrew children, young teenagers who made a choice not to bow their knee to anything or anyone except the Lord God, Jehovah. Because they refused, they were thrown into a fiery furnace. With ropes on their hands, as the king and his strong men looked inside, they saw four in the furnace, and one looked like the Son of God.

I reminded them, "Obedience to God was more important than anything else. God saw their faith and delivered them from certain death." I told them, "I am certain this simple obedience will move the hand of God and He will come to our rescue."

Four days later, the day I call "showdown day," was a day that will live in our memories forever. The three of us—Barbara, Tamara, and I arrived at the doctor's building without the paid receipts we had been asked to bring for reimbursement from the Muscular Dystrophy Foundation. We entered the medical facility and stepped into the elevator that carried us to the fourth floor. Tamara refused to use a wheelchair. Her determination to walk on her own two feet was unchangeable even though she suffered agonizing pain with each step. She scooted her feet with unflinching surrender as we exited the elevator.

I walked backwards so I could look into the face of one of the most courageous human beings I had ever known. She and I talked each step of the way. I sensed that today would be a day like no other, telling her that today was showdown day. I declared, "Tamara, it's God's Word against medical science. They say you are going to die; His Word says you will be healed."

I looked at her with swatches of hair missing because it had fallen out, her thin arms drawn upward and all but useless, scooting her feet with legs that she could hardly lift. She struggled to place one foot in front of the other. I said, "You do not look healed to me, and I do not know how or when, but I do know you will be healed soon."

It took awhile, but we reached the doctor's office. The receptionist greeted us cordially and inquired, "Mr. Youngblood, did you bring the receipts?" She informed me of the only good news she knew—we would not have to pay for today's visit nor the final tests scheduled to be administered.

I reached into my pocket and produced a signed check. I looked at her and said, "Today we will be paying for the office visit and all costs of the test performed. We will not qualify for medical relief provided for those who have MD."

She was stunned at my reply. She placed the check to one side of her work station and said, "I'll hold it until a later time."

We were scheduled to meet, for the first time, the head physician of this elite medical team. He would administer the final test necessary to complete their files. The test was called an EMG. Finally, after sitting in the examination room for a period of time, the doctor entered and greeted us politely. He began to scan through the file compiled over the past five months. He looked up at us, his dark eyes filled with sad concern, and said, "I am sorry you have MD."

Referring to Tamara's great-grandfather, who had died in less than one year after a diagnosis of muscular dystrophy, he explained that it was not uncommon for this deadly disease to skip to the third generation. This doctor from India was the finest and most sensitive of any who had attended Tamara.

He spoke in gentle words, "The monitor sitting on the cabinet will show and produce a graph through an electrical response that will occur when needles are placed approximately two inches apart into your body from your hips to the tops of your feet. As the needles are placed into you, an electrical charge will be sent one to the other to reveal the severed nervous system that covers the entire body."

This was *not* what I wanted to hear. I turned to him and said, "So this monitor will say my daughter is going to die!" Not waiting for his reply, I turned and pointed my finger at the machine and spoke out loud, saying, "In the name of Jesus, I rebuke you and defy you to show me my daughter has MD." I turned, looking at the face of this stunned and bewildered physician, and said, "Let's begin."

It took the doctor a minute to gather his composure, and then he explained to Tamara about the pain she would experience during this twenty-minute procedure. He assured her that even grown men have cried out. He gently told her it was okay for her to cry or scream. Halfway through this terrible test, as I sat beside her holding her hand, I saw one tear escape her eye and roll down her cheek. No screams or crying. This began to unnerve the doctor and he interrupted the procedure asking, "Tamara, do you want something to drink?"

"No, I'm okay," she said. "Let's get this over with."

Once the test was complete, the doctor left the room, notifying us that within thirty minutes the results would be read to us in another room. Thirty minutes can seem like an eternity. Thankfully, the other room had windows, so we could see outside.

We turned as we heard the door open and a woman physician, who had been involved with Tamara's care every step of the way, walked in. She held in her hand the file that contained the final test and all the procedures done in the last five months. She walked over to the windows and stood there looking out. I sensed she didn't want to look at us.

She began to explain the excellence of this medical team and their careful diagnosis. "We have shared our work with other specialists and the laboratories we have worked with, and all agree and conclude Tamara has MD."

I was quickly becoming frustrated with her long, drawn out review and bluntly asked, "What is it you are trying to say?"

She slowly turned to face us, and with tears in her eyes she said, "Yesterday Tamara had MD; today she does not."

Her words will ring in my ears as long as I live!

It was as if her eyes were staring into the emptiness of space with this blank look, and then she spoke again, "I don't know what happened, neither do I know the answer."

I was amazed at her statements and replied, "The answer is Jesus, the Christ."

Startled, she looked at me and said, "I do not believe in Him."

I guess it was my turn to be stunned. I looked at this precious woman with sadness in my heart. I spoke the truth to her. "Whether you believe in Him or not does not change what has happened. The reason Tamara is healed is because we do believe in Him!"

"So," I asked the physician, "what do we do now?"

She looked bewildered and said, "I do not know! I suppose we need to see Tamara in two weeks and see what's happening then."

Tamara slowly rose to her feet and left the room, scooting out to the receptionist desk. The receptionist smiled at us and said, "I've already heard the wonderful news," and she handed me the bill for the office visit. I filled in the amount of the check, very pleased that there would be no refund from any foundation!

The appointment was set for two weeks later. We would return for a blood test to measure the muscle inflammation in Tamara's body. Three days later, at 7:30 A.M., I opened the door to her bedroom and to my surprise, she was sitting up on the side of the bed, fully dressed and smiling.

"Who helped you get dressed?" I asked her.

Proudly, she said, "No one. I did it myself."

For the rest of the two-week period, every day we celebrated as Tamara stepped onto a fast track to full recovery.

When it was time for blood work again, it was like skyrockets on Fourth of July. The results showed a reduction from 2130 points of muscle inflammation down to 280 points.

Another appointment in two weeks showed even more progress.

Tamara celebrated her freedom as her feet that once scooted walked briskly into the doctor's office. Smiling, she turned toward the examination room. Having been there many times before, she lifted her arm and extended it so they could draw blood. The bombs begin bursting with air rockets exploding within our hearts as we heard that the score of muscle inflammation had fallen from 2130 points to an average person's normal level of 225 points.

We won and MD suffered defeat! Within three months, Tamara had improved enough to go back to her cheerleading squad.

Five years later, this same elite medical team declared Tamara, "disease free . . . a miracle."

Today Tamara and her husband have three beautiful children. She is thirty-nine years old and has been in perfect health since that Showdown Day!

During the editing of this book Tamara read this chapter and wanted to share a few words with you, the reader:

"For me, this was a time of acceptance or non-acceptance of my situation. I did do my best to hide my pain and shield my symptoms from those I loved as much as possible. Reality for me was what it was, and I did my very best not to let it interfere with my real life. I know it sounds weird, but I was detached from the diagnosis. I just took what came, one day at a time. It's how I had to live!

"I had an odd inner peace in the midst of the storm. I really hoped I had accomplished all I was created for. It was not this way for my parents! I think they tried to hide as much of their own pain as possible from me. Reading this chapter made me remember so much of God's mercy and love, but also made me remember how much I hid from as many as possible—including hiding the hurt from my parents.

"My greatest fear became the concern that if the house caught on fire, I would not be able to get out of bed by myself and I would die there! My nightly prayer became more about my house not catching on fire than for my healing.

"I did my best to keep my friends from noticing, but many times during lunch at school, I leaned down—not under the table but as close as possible without causing a scene—and pushed my food down my throat with my fingers because the muscles in my throat weren't strong enough to swallow my food. I almost hated lunchtime because there was always a risk I would choke and be unable to breathe. It was very frightening and embarrassing for me.

"At school my cousin, Delania, offered to carry me on her back. I might have given in once or twice for laughs. I remember those steep stairs in the building and how we were excused from our tardiness since we had to wait until the stairs cleared to even begin our trek up them!

"I still have homecoming pictures that make my eyes water when I see them. I was not in any pretty physical state. I only can attribute what I see now in those pictures to what I saw in the mirror then—the Lord gave me blindness to my own physical appearance in such a way that I didn't see what others saw! I truly believe it was His way of protecting me.

"I am so thankful to all my friends who lovingly assured me and supported me through those rough days. Thanks for the memories and for loving me through it all!

"God is *so good* and incredibly faithful to me and my family!"

CHAPTER 12

HOPE FOR THE HOPELESS

When did it all start and where was its beginning? Was it thirty years ago in Grand Prairie, Texas, when a small, helpless woman was dealt blow after brutal blow by the devil called Betrayal? A devil who would deceive her husband, drag him down into the depths of moral failure, and cause him to abandon her and their four children and leave them alone at the mercy of the beasts called Fear and Death?

She must have been desperate to call and ask me for counsel, as if I would know what she should do. She asked me, "Is there any way you could possibly help me?" Sitting there watching her hands tremble, I didn't have a clue what to tell her or how to fix this terrible mess.

I sat in my office looking across the room at my sister-in-law, Joan Vandergriff, only thirty-two years old. A short time ago she had been an attractive, secure, married woman with a twinkle in her eyes and a smile that lit up her face, revealing a radiance of confidence and joy. How quickly her countenance had changed! Her face was now shadowed in darkness, seized by the merciless beast. Her eyes once twinkled; now they were consumed by desperation. The smile I remembered was gone from her lips and the words she spoke were slurred, hardly audible.

Shaking, she told me of the voices that reasoned with her, saying, "You have no way of providing for your four children, making house and car payments, paying for utilities, education, and medical needs. . . ." She trailed off as if she was listening again to the voices, repeatedly giving her the list few people could provide for, much less a divorced woman who had never held a job other than being a homemaker for all the years of her marriage.

The spirit of fear spoke endless words of hopelessness that sent wave after wave of panic through her mind, bringing mass confusion into her troubled soul. I watched her as she fought to breathe. It was as if a giant anaconda had grabbed her and was squeezing the very life out of her.

A short time later, with the limited advice I had given her, she prepared for bed. In her nightgown, grasping the Bible in her hand, she looked at this holy book. She recalled being raised all of her life in a God-fearing home. Her father, Junior Lee, was a minister and pastor of a local church, and her mother, Azell, was a studious reader of the Word of God. Together they studied the Scriptures and held fast to them in both the good and the difficult times.

As an adult, the desperate circumstances Joan faced compelled her to try out this God for herself. Despondent and realizing she was alone, she remembered what her parents had done in frightening situations.

While her four children slept in their beds, Joan picked up her Bible and opened it slowly to see just where its pages might fall.

She looked down and her weary eyes began to read a covenant the faithful God Himself spoke, saying,

> Do not be afraid; you will not suffer shame. Do not fear disgrace; you will not be humiliated. You will forget the shame of your youth and remember no more the reproach of your widowhood. For your Maker is your husband—the Lord Almighty is his name. The Holy One of Israel is your Redeemer, he is called the God of all the earth. The Lord will call you back as if you were a wife deserted and distressed in spirit—a wife who married young, only to be rejected, says your God.
>
> —Isaiah 54:4–6

In this moment it was as if God Himself spoke aloud to her. His voice jarred her to her feet and she recalled the old song the congregation at her father's church sang many times, "Standing on the Promises of God." For the first time in her life, she took those words literally. She laid the Bible down on the floor and stepped carefully on top of these tried and true words of God.

I can see her now, standing alone in her nightgown, reaching through her desperation and clinging to one last hope—her *stand* upon the Word of God.

Awakened early the next morning by a sound in the distance, she realized she had slept better than she had in a very long time. She struggled to her feet, grasping and groping in the dark. Finally, she located the source of the noise. Relieved that it was only the alarm clock she had set for 6:15 A.M. and shutting it off, she rushed into the kitchen to make the children's lunches and prepare breakfast for her four children.

Once the kids were on their way to school, Joan found herself alone again. The quietness of an empty house gave the opportunity for the voices in her head to crank up in volume. Their topic continued as before. Their chants of gloom and doom, hopelessness and despair drove her to open her Bible. Again, she turned the pages and an amazing story seemed to leap into her spirit as she read the story of Elisha, the prophet, and the widow who cried out to him in her desperation.

The widow's husband was dead. She had no money and in exchange for debts she owed, the creditors were coming to take away her two sons, who would become their slaves in exchange for debts. The great prophet instructed her to look around her house to see what she had. Feeling desperate, she said, "I have nothing but a little oil" (2 Kings 4:1–2 NIV).

As Joan finished reading this ancient story, she heard a voice prompting her to look around her kitchen to see what she had that God could use. Then she saw it! A metal rack containing a small bottle of herbs, with an old orange label on it, was sitting nearby. Desperately, she grabbed it and held it to her heart. She cried out to God, "What should I do with these herbs?" She waited breathlessly for an answer, wondering—what is God trying to tell me?

One morning, anxiety drove her to look out her kitchen window. *What is it I'm supposed to see?* Her eyes searched the side yard, and she noticed the dandelions growing wildly in her overgrown yard. Leaning over the window sill, she was mesmerized at the beauty of a small, indiscreet flower.

Is this the answer I desperately need? How ridiculous could this be? she thought. What could she do with a useless, weed-like flower no one would want, much less buy? Unable to escape the voice that had impressed the bottle of herbs on her heart and brought the dandelions to her mind, she wondered if this was a miracle God was sending to her—the solution that would meet all of her financial needs. Her hopes skyrocketed as she hurried to finish cleaning the kitchen.

Joan knew she must find the answer to this mystery of the dandelions. On her way to the public library only a few miles away, she meditated on the value of this bottle of herbs. She had been giving herbs to her youngest son, Darin, as a natural remedy for his asthma.

Arriving, she hurried through the library doors. Her search began immediately in the area of medicine. Who would know more than Hippocrates, the father of medicine? This great doctor utilized nineteen different herbs in his profession and coined the famous quote, "A wise man ought to say health is his most valuable possession."

Her excitement built as she became more and more convinced herbs could hold the answer for many health needs. Then to her surprise, she found it. She began to read about the dandelion flowers which spring up every year. It too is an herb. That did it!

Pictures in her mind flashed with fields of dandelions, bottles of herbs, faces of her kinfolks, neighbors, and friends. It was all right there in front of her eyes. Her plan was simple and her expectations were low. She only had enough faith to step out in the new venture and order two bottles of dandelion. She would make copies of the information acquired at the library concerning herbs. Immediately, she called her sisters, friends, and neighbors and asked if she could come to their houses and share this exciting news—that God provided healing, naturally, through herbs that grow freely from the earth.

Her excitement took a nosedive when she realized how limited this new venture was with an inventory of just two bottles of herbs. Then she heard a voice reminding her of how God had increased the widow's oil. Encouraged again, she made a phone call to Nature's Sunshine to inform them of their new employee and said she wanted to make her first big splash into the company by ordering two bottles of herbs for her first Nature Sunshine party! Can you just imagine the thoughts of the person on the other end of the line as he yelled, "Two bottles of herbs for Joan Vandergriff, our brand new manager from the great state of Texas"?

I think all of us can understand why she imagined everyone was laughing—everyone but me, her brother-in-law, because the third party was to be at our house and this meant, *I'm out of here!* What in the world is an herb party anyway?

No one really knew she had already received her first miracle when she opened the box from Nature Sunshine products. Expecting to find two bottles of herbs, she was surprised to find that the shipment contained twenty. God had already begun to multiply the oil for Joan, just as He did in the ancient story of the widow and the prophet.

The same two feet that took their stand on the promises of God late one night in Grand Prairie, Texas, would carry her around the world to more than forty countries and to cities throughout the United States—not just as a sightseer, but as a representative of Nature's Sunshine. Joan became a celebrated educational speaker, who stood before thousands of its members from thirty-eight countries.

Thousands of eyes followed her as she walked upon the platform lined with alternative medicine doctors of many nations. Her beautiful feet, which had stood on the Bible that night, carried her to becoming number three in the United States of Nature Sunshine's 8,000 managers, in a company with more than 750,000 distributors worldwide with 21,000 members in Texas alone.

I can almost see him now; this same young man who took the order for those two bottles of herbs, writing out thousands of orders for Energ-V, which contains ten different herbs in one capsule and is named after its originator, Joan Vandergriff.

If only I had known, my one wish would have been to go with her to the country of Peru where she was escorted from the airport by the presidential motorcade and she was a guest speaker before the Congress of Alternative Medicine with more than 1,000 doctors in attendance. Had I been there, I would have placed behind the podium her old worn Bible, opened to the scriptures where God said, "Do not be afraid; you will not suffer shame. Do not fear disgrace; you will not be humiliated. You will forget the shame of your youth and remember no more the reproach of your widowhood. For your Maker is your husband—the Lord Almighty is His name," for her to stand on.

Every life is a journey! Only God knows the distance we will travel and the paths we will take. There are times we are blessed, as if soaring on wings of eagles, ascending to the tops of the mountains where we can breathe in the refreshing aroma of mighty pine trees and catch the tantalizing smell of mountain cedar. There, for a wondrous moment, we can look down on the hills and valleys below and at a distance see a deer drinking from a glistening, flowing stream with a rainbow trout waiting behind every pebble. It is in these times, with hearts of gratitude, we can witness and acknowledge the wonderful works and the living presence of our great God, the Creator, and possibly, just maybe we will hear His voice.

Quickly, too quickly, we descend into the valleys and the desert places below where we fall prey to the enormity of life's challenges. As our troubles begin to multiply, we become overwhelmed by the multitude of voices speaking inside our minds.

The thoughts of guilt or failure and words of destruction propelled by wave after wave of panic attacks leave us in a state of despair and hopelessness. We grasp, as one who is drowning, for a straw of hope for rescue. Somehow, among all the voices, if at those times we could recognize the voice of God, we could be saved from all of our troubles.

Eleven years had passed since Joan had sat in my office asking for counsel. During these eventful years, God kept His promise of being a "husband to the widow and supplying all of her needs." He enabled her to rise to the top of her profession in the world of alternative medicine, which had provided her with more than enough income to send all four children through college. But one night the beast called the spirit of fear had grabbed her again, taunting and tormenting her mind.

Barbara and I were asleep when I heard what seemed like a strange sound. I wondered, *Is it a telephone ringing in this deep, dark, deserted tunnel I am in?* Startled by my wife's voice asking, "Are you going to answer it?" I reached to answer the phone, hearing Joan's voice on the line.

Dathan, her oldest son, had been driving under the influence of alcohol at 2:00 A.M. He veered into the wrong lane and hit, head-on, another automobile carrying five teenagers. Three were flown to different hospitals, all in extreme critical condition. One was in a coma, her life hanging by a thread. The District Attorney was waiting to file criminal charges of involuntary manslaughter pending the outcome of a blood alcohol test and the death of even one of these precious children.

Joan continued her sad story, telling me that one week ago in a heated confrontation Dathan had told her loud and clear, "I will never be saved! I will never go to your kind of church! I will never be what you want me to be! Stop praying for me!"

Emotionally crushed and realizing how helpless she was, Joan fell on her knees and cried out to the One and only God of heaven, "Father, he is in your hands. Whatever it takes to bring him to You, do it!"

Her story continued and she told me he was at that point in full-blown rebellion. For five years he had refused to enter through the doors of any church. The need to feel good drove him to extreme alcohol and drug abuse. It took all of these for Dathan to cope with the loss of his father, the one man he loved and adored.

Not wanting to hear any more, I interrupted Joan, "What is it you want me to do?"

Traumatized, her voice shaking, she said, "I have no one else to turn to! Dathan has reached a place in his life where he has little respect for anyone. I don't think he will listen to anyone except you, his 'Uncle Alan.'" Agonizing, she continued, "I know you hear from God and will do what ever He tells you to do. Is it possible for you to come to my house and talk to Dathan?"

On the other end of the receiver, Joan wasn't aware that I, too, was having my own nightmare from hell. The economy had taken a massive nosedive and with it the world of real estate— my world—lay in total ruins. For me, it was as if the earth had opened up and swallowed everything Barbara and I had worked for all of our lives. It had devoured our bank accounts, our construction company, and even our confidence in our identity as to who we are and, worse yet—who God really is.

Everywhere I turned, I heard voices mocking me, accusing me, telling me all of it was my fault. I became the brunt of the blame for every single failure we experienced daily. I could smell the pending doom as the losses marched endlessly into my life. It was like a monstrous military invasion from the prince of the power of the air and the rulers of the darkness, all on a mission to steal, kill, and destroy everything. The loss of the sum of who I am, what I had, or who I would ever become, caused me to stumble down the slippery slope of depression, sliding faster and deeper, totally out of control.

I saw the road signs at every turn. They spoke as if they had voices, saying, "Danger, foreclosures, bankruptcy, and destruction ahead." But at last I came to the end of that horrific, mind-bending plunge. A voice whispered in my ear. It was subtle, non-threatening, and sensible, trying to convince me of a plan for how I could escape from the nightmare. Finally, a rescue plan that made sense! For me to escape only required my participation; otherwise, the plan would not work.

Listening intently to this unidentified voice, I tried to determine who was speaking to me. It sounded so good that it made me think, *This must be the way to heaven. All I have to do is obey; then I'll find peace and rest for my troubled soul.*

I followed this soothing voice, each step bringing me closer to the end of my journey. Then, as if in a vision, I noticed on the left side of the dusty road an old wooden sign shaped like an arrow with a word written in faded letters: "Danger."

Coming to a complete stop, I saw an old filling station with one pump. It reminded me of one I had seen when I was twelve or thirteen years old. Traveling to California, we had been headed for Disneyland®. Dad had chosen a path that would take us through the desert. For the last twenty miles we saw signs along the side of the road with the same repetitive message: "Warning: Last chance for gas, food, and water." But something caught my eye—something different. The front door of the old station stood partially open. I could see the rays of a bright light shining from the inside.

Clearly, I heard a voice speaking, "Come unto me, you who are weary and I will give you rest." I froze; not even a muscle was moving, and I was certain I had heard these words before. *Could it be my kinsman Redeemer; my One and only Savior?*

As I struggled with what I should do, the voice spoke again. This time it was loud and clear, shaking me to my senses. It sounded as if it came from the open door of the old gas station. The words I heard still echo in my ears. "Your life is not yours to take. You have already surrendered it to me and now it is only yours to give for others."

My thoughts were interrupted by the same voice who spoke to the dead carcass of Lazarus when Christ raised him from the dead. He commanded, "Tell her you will be there tomorrow night."

Startled, I blurted out, "Joan, I will be there at seven o'clock tomorrow evening."

She gasped softly and said, "Wow, that was quick!"

Wanting to get off the phone, I instructed her, "Do not tell a soul concerning this conversation and most certainly, not Dathan. Barbara and I will see you tomorrow night."

God looked into my heart and reminded me of the words He had spoken to His disciples: "My command is this: love each other as I have loved you. Greater love has no one than this; that he lay down his life for his friends" (John 15:12–13 NIV).

Today, Joan Vandergriff, N.D., is a traditional naturopath and natural health educator, who found wellness after suffering an intestinal parasitic infection and liver damage. She is a Certified Nutritional Health Practitioner (C.N.H.P.), certified

Master Herbalist (M.H.), and Certified Iridologist by Dr. Bernard Jensen. She has been working with clients for over thirty-two years and was part of a medical team researching Lyme's disease in 2002 and 2006 using Ph balancing. She is a popular convention speaker and the celebrated author of *Nature's Treasure Chest*, which contains 360 health recipes and has sold over 350,000 copies to date.

Joan lives to minister hope to the hopeless and healing to the nations.

CHAPTER 13

ORION—MIGHTY WARRIOR

Prompted by the voice of my Commander-in-Chief, who had not lost confidence in me, the rules of engagement were well defined. They were confidential and clothed in secrecy. It was to be a surprise attack to free Dathan, the hostage, and inflict heavy damage on his captor, leaving him unable to ever return. After receiving my orders, I struggled to my feet, realizing the mission to rescue another was far more important than the wounds of battle I had suffered.

Yes, I had been bombarded by the enemy from land, sea, and sky, but God's banner of love still waved over me. The onslaught of the adversary left me bloodied but un-bowed. The forces of this present life had battered me, but I remained un-broken. Every time the enemy wanted to write me off, I always answered the call and at no time have I ever backed down.

The rulers of darkness had made a tactical blunder by thinking I was alone. They had underestimated my dependence on the heavenly Trio Who lived inside me. With my will unified with theirs, we would not be defeated. I knew that that night we would rout the enemy!

The element of surprise proved to be the undoing of the demons who raged inside Dathan. When we arrived at Joan's, to keep her and Barbara "out of harm's way," I quietly instructed them to stay in another part of the house and not come out until I called for them. Joan directed me with hand motions to the bedroom where he was. As I entered the room, the television was blaring; it was the middle of March and college basketball was in full swing. It was the time of the year called March Madness.

My sudden appearance was a surprise. Dathan looked somewhat startled as he lay there with a broken right leg and his life shattered. My greeting was friendly as I casually told him I had just come by to see him. Somewhat bewildered by my arrival, he turned and continued watching the basketball game. So I would not play my hand, I sat down near his bed and joined him in watching the game. The Texas Longhorns were in the heat of battle, fighting as the underdog against a superior team. I am a hook-em-horns fan, so I quickly became a cheerleader for them.

Fifteen or twenty minutes passed. I was caught up in Texas' fight for survival when my Commanding Officer's voice interrupted me. He said, "Shut it off! This is not the reason I sent you here!" I stood immediately and said to Dathan, "Cut off the television. I didn't come to watch the game with you."

Dathan turned to look at me, and I could see the depth of despondency in his dark brown eyes. Not only was he in intense pain from his shattered leg, but he was also distraught with the knowledge that it would be many months before he could walk and even longer before he could return to work to earn desperately needed money. Worried sick about the possibilities of one of the teenagers dying, which would lead to his arrest, he also faced possible court appearances that were all alcohol related. He lay there feeling completely trapped like an animal, caught in a snare without any possibility of escape, festering with bitterness and hatred he had harbored deep within his chest for years.

I looked at Dathan with pity, but with hatred for the demons that held him captive and used him as their slave. Dazed by my command, he turned off the television. I began, "Dathan, I've come so you might go free. I have been sent by the God Who loves you—the same God you are angry at and hate. Inside of you a strong man lives and he is holding you as his captive. Tonight, he will be forced to let you go and forever release his hold on you. The power of God is more powerful than any devil who rules in your heart. His truth will set you free!"

Gazing deeper into his eyes, I saw an innocent victim held by a vicious intruder who had taken advantage of him while he was still a child. It wasn't something of his doing. He had been wounded by different people at various times, leaving him reeking with bitterness and hatred. This old devil had taken full control of his life, dictating his every thought.

Was he angry? Oh, yes, he was angry—with anger brought on by the frustration of not knowing how to escape. The feelings of loneliness set in like a sickness, ruling his life as he slowly submitted to his captivity, even to the point where he believed God *could* rescue him but *would not*.

Now it was my turn to be angry! I exposed the voice of the lying imposter, telling Dathan, "Tonight, not only has God sent me, but God Himself has come to set you free from all of the hurts you have suffered." While speaking those words, I laid my hand on his chest, and then with a loud voice I said, "In the name of Jesus of Nazareth, I command every devil which holds you to loose you and let you go."

As I continued praying, Dathan reached down with his hand, putting it on his stomach as he began to feel the presence of God touch his heart. I stood there amazed as the mighty power of this glorious God changed the countenance of Dathan right before my eyes. I spoke tenderly to Dathan, my nephew, telling him God was ready to forgive him. All he had to do was ask. Tears flowed down his face and his lips quivered. He said, "God, I am so sorry. Please forgive me of all of my sins."

I felt like I could hear all of heaven breaking out in total celebration—a precious son had come home. Dathan relaxed and lay back comfortably on his pillow, his face aglow with peace and joy.

Looking at him, I was proud of Dathan! I bent over the side of the bed where he lay and hugged him, telling him I loved him. With one more glance at his radiant face, I left the room to find his mother and my wife.

Instructing Joan, "Go into the bedroom first, and Barbara and I will follow close behind." As she entered the room, Dathan reached both of his thin arms toward her, crying unashamed, and said, "Mama, I am sorry, please will you forgive me?"

My sister-in-law turned toward me in total amazement, asking, "What have you done to my son?"

Looking at her with compassion, I said, "Your son was dead but now he is alive!"

In our presence mother and son held each other and wept tears of joy, as Barbara and I slipped quietly out of the room. We stood on their large front porch and breathed in deep breaths of fresh spring air, exhaling all of the poisonous anxieties from our lungs. Gazing up at God's beautiful heaven with too many twinkling stars to count, we lovingly smiled at each other.

Tonight Dathan was free! Much to my surprise, I, too, had taken a giant step toward my freedom. Little did we know that one day Dathan would become a minister of the gospel of Christ and the senior pastor of the church he had turned his back on.

Barbara was at the wheel of our Chevrolet® Suburban, driving us toward our home in Colleyville. It was such a wonderful sight to see a mother and her beloved son embracing each other. Their tears of joy flowed down their faces and their hearts abounded with loving gratitude toward their heavenly Father, Who is faithful to keep all of His promises, imparts us with His grace, and floods us with His undying love. What an exhilarating night it had been!

We had fought the enemy in hand-to-hand combat, taking from him the spoils, inflicting heavy blows upon him, and causing him to suffer from the brutal beating we had rained upon his head. I felt certain he had crawled back into his cave, there to lick his wounds. I enjoyed recalling the fight we had just won, blow by blow. Ah, victory is so sweet!

As I savored each tasty morsel of our victorious triumph, Barbara pulled into the driveway of our home. Exhausted physically, but emotionally floating on air, I made a quick stop at the pantry in the kitchen for a midnight snack and then went to the refrigerator for a tall glass of milk. (Yes, nothing is smoother going down than ice-cold milk!)

At last, it was time for bed. Grabbing the staircase rail, hand over hand we pulled our weary legs up the steps. Though our legs seem heavy, our hearts were as light as a handful of feathers. Finally, the clock was set for 6:30 A.M. and the lights were all off. With hugs, kisses, and goodnights given to one and all, with a smile on my face and peace in my heart, everything seemed well.

Within minutes, I sensed myself drifting off into a deep sleep. Was I dreaming, or was this an emotional roller coaster I was on? What a ride it was giving me at breathtaking speeds, plunging down this deep dark tunnel. It seemed I was careening out of control, around the curves, trying desperately to hold on to something.

There was an occasional glimpse of the abyss, and then I felt myself slammed against its stony walls, tearing the flesh from my bones. I heard screams coming from the damned as they groped in the darkness of their minds and the depths of their hopelessness, finding no way to escape.

Then suddenly, I burst out of the tunnel into a dry, barren land, parched by the heat of a scorching sun that is much too close to the earth. My tongue stuck, swollen, to the roof of my mouth; I was so thirsty, but there was no water! The hot desert sand blasted me by the scorching winds of time. It felt as if my very flesh was melting.

When it seemed I would perish, at that moment I was catapulted up, up, and away over the top of the mountains, above the storm clouds of life, past the pinnacle of where the eagles fly. Without effort I soared and glided above all my problems as they disappeared from my view. All of a sudden, my exhilarating ride came abruptly to an end, and I heard someone or something coming up the steps to our room. *Am I dreaming?* My head was spinning. I remembered I was exhausted. I must have gone sound asleep!

Jolted to my senses, I looked at the clock on the nightstand. Its illuminated numbers displayed 2:10 A.M. I could hear someone outside our closed bedroom door. My natural instinct was to jump up and grab the door before he did and hit him head on with a body block. Sitting up in bed, it felt like my lower body was paralyzed from the waist down. Frozen in position, I was unable to move. As the door of my bedroom opened slowly, I reached as far as I could for the light to turn it on.

As I did, I saw him oozing through the door! It was a behemoth beast; he was grotesque, ugly, and frightening! Obese, horribly obese, possibly weighing six or seven hundred pounds of fat flab, roll after roll—all rotting flesh, hanging from his dirty, yellow-looking body. As he moved closer to my bed, I noticed he had no arms, only two stubs protruding from his shoulders.

Horrified, I could hear the wooden floor popping under the weight of this monster, and I recognized the spirit of fear and death. *What is he doing?* I fell back on my bed, terrified with fear as I looked at his face. He was a monster, with his right eye large and hanging down. His left eye was gone, with nothing but a gaping, festering hole where an eye should have been. Noises escaped his large pig-like nose. Mystified, I noticed the strangest thing of all. His mouth was partially open, with ugly thin lips revealing that he did not have any teeth. He was toothless!

The beast looked down at me and commenced to crawl on top of my paralyzed body. His weight was immense, causing the bed to sag. As he began to wallow on top of me, my blood pressure seemed to explode in my head and my body instantly began to sweat profusely. I could not breathe—he was crushing the very life out of me.

In my panic, I thought, *My God, he is going to kill me.* With my last breath, I gasped out the name, "Jesus!" Instantly, the monster rose up and lurked by the side of my bed. That's when I saw a radiant glow of translucent light filling the room. The ugly beast was as astonished as I was! Staring in amazement, I saw the most awesome celestial being ever imaginable standing at the foot of my bed! He stood eight or nine feet tall, possibly weighing four hundred plus pounds. His radiant face was ruddy, strong, and powerful—glowing from the inside out. His hair was woven with gold and silver strands, falling gently onto his shoulders. He was adorned in armor made of gold, highlighted with lights twinkling like stars or diamonds. At his side was a sword; its beauty was beyond imagination.

Astonished, I sat up in bed wide awake, wondering who he was. This magnificent heavenly being must have read my mind. At that moment his large lips moved as he spoke. "I am Orion. I have been sent to rescue you!"

Relieved, I turned to see that the spirit of fear and death had already left the room, never to return. I can only describe my feelings with one word, "Stunned!" I watched this beautiful, celestial, heavenly being disappear right before my eyes.

God had sent a mighty warrior angel named Orion to rescue me from my enemy, the spirit of fear and death!

I lay there meditating upon the wonders of this amazing God Whose ways are perfect. My thoughts are the same as now. It is impossible to measure the magnitude of this magnificent intrinsic, Living God Whose name is above every name.

With the image of this wonderful, celestial God flooding my mind, I drifted off into blissful, heavenly slumber.

Awakening the next morning, I made my way down the same stairs the grotesque behemoth spirit of fear had climbed just hours before. Now he had been exposed as a fake, blubbering beast without arms and with an ugly mouth with no teeth. Never again will he strike fear in me! If he knocks on my door, I will rebuke him in the mighty name of Jesus and he will flee.

Smelling the tantalizing scents of fresh coffee, bacon, and eggs coming from the kitchen, I quickened my steps to the breakfast table. I leaned over and kissed my wife, who had begun to eat without me. Sitting there, sipping coffee from her favorite marbleized green mug, she lowered it from her lips. Smiling, she quietly said, "I wasn't sure you heard me call ten minutes ago. Sorry, I started eating without you."

Pleasantly, I looked at her, returning her smile and sitting down next to her. "Honey, I'm going to tell you the most incredible story, which happened last night. You go ahead and finish eating while I share with you every detail that took place while you were sleeping."

For the next forty-five minutes, I related to her the incredible story of the celestial angel, Orion, who appeared in our room in the nighttime. Barbara sat there, stunned and speechless but greatly intrigued by the mighty angel who had come to my rescue. Finally, being able to speak, she mused, "Are you going to tell this to anyone?"

Looking at her, I carefully replied, "That's part of the reason for my tardiness this morning. I lay there debating who else I would tell beside you."

"Well, is there someone else we know who would believe this?" she replied.

"I'm not comfortable sharing this with many people, but tonight there is a person I feel compelled to tell about this encounter," I continued.

Her eyes widened as she questioned, "Who?"

Taking a deep breath, I spoke. "Remember, tonight a group of musicians and vocalists are coming over to prepare for Sunday morning. I'm thinking of telling the story to Pat Smith."

She paused for a moment, pondering this in her mind before she spoke. "I believe he will be the perfect one."

Relieved by her confirmation, I looked forward to the evening. What a joyful time it would be—two hours of music and praise!

After the practice came to a celebratory end, I slipped over and whispered into Pat's ear, "Can you stay awhile and talk with me?"

Always cordial and available to me, he quickly said, "I have all night if you need it."

Retiring into my office behind closed doors and relaxing on the burgundy leather sofa, I began to share the incredible story of the spirit of fear and the wondrous appearing of the mighty angel, Orion. As I described every detail as I had seen him, Pat's countenance lit up with a big smile stretching across his face.

With his eyes twinkling, he said, "You don't know who Orion is, do you?"

Looking at him, I questioned, "That name, Orion, I've never heard before, have you?"

He answered joyfully, "Pastor Alan, for years I studied astronomy and astrology. What is interesting to me is that you named my favorite constellation and described its configuration of stars precisely."

I looked at him, more confused than ever. "Pat, you lost me! I've never been a student of astronomy or astrology. What has any of this to do with a mighty angel named Orion?"

The smile never left his face as he explained, "I only wish you had a telescope. We would go out on your balcony and I would show you exactly where the constellation Orion is located on the equator east of Taurus. He is viewed as the mightiest warrior of the celestial heavens, wearing a belt with a sword."

Once again, I was stunned as severely by his words as I had been when I saw the angel Orion standing at the end of my bed. Pat looked at me, saying, "I can understand that you don't study astronomy nor dabble in astrology, but you, being a student of the Word, should recognize the name Orion from the Bible."

I stopped him, saying, "You mean Orion is in the Bible?"

He replied, "Yes, in two or three places."

Reaching instantly across my desk, I handed him my black leather Bible and, almost doubtful, I demanded, "Show me!"

He proudly took my worn Bible and turned knowingly to one of the oldest books of the Bible, Job. Speaking of God and His creation, it says, "He alone stretches out the heavens, and treads on the waves of the sea. He is the maker of the Bear and Orion, the Pleiades and the constellations of the South, He performs wonders that cannot be fathomed, miracles that cannot be counted" (Job 9:8–10 NIV).

Sitting there and looking at Pat in complete astonishment, I spoke the only words that came to me, "Amazing!"

I will never cease to be in a state of wonder at this awesome, mysterious, marvelous, and Living God, Who truly performs wonders that cannot be fathomed and miracles no man can count. My mind can't comprehend the magnitude of this great and mighty God, Who, without ceasing, has continued revealing Himself to me, proving Himself as my greatest friend and constant companion. He had come down into my world and shared His world with me!

CHAPTER 14

ANGELS ON ASSIGNMENT

If you make the Most High your dwelling—even the Lord, who is my refuge—then no harm will befall you, no disaster will come near your tent. For he will command his angels concerning you to guard you in all your ways.

—Psalm 91:9–11 NIV

I can still hear my mother's trembling voice scream out into the darkness after midnight, as she sat up in her bed in the back bedroom of their modest frame house. Still clutching the rose-pink blanket with her left hand, she violently shook my elderly father, trying to awaken him out of his deep sleep. Being unable to arouse him immediately increased the panic that raged within her, causing her to scream out all the louder.

"Irvin, Irvin, there's a man in the house!"

This scenario occurred many times throughout their sixty years of marriage, when my mother awakened him in the night because she was frightened of sounds or dreams. As he rose up to respond to her terrified voice, his typical response to her was, "Lay down, Irene, and be quiet! There's no one in the house except you and me. Go back to sleep. I have to go to work at 5:30 A.M."

The penetrating sound of a telephone ringing broke into my early morning slumber. Groggily, I raised my head and glanced first toward the bedroom window to see the early morning glow of the rising sun on the horizon. With anxiety building in my mind, I wondered who could be calling at the beginning of a new day.

Clearing my throat from early morning hoarseness, I croaked out roughly, "Hello."

An old, familiar voice responded, "Son, it's your dad. Your mama and I want you to come to the house today. We've got a great story to tell you!"

Hesitantly, he struggled, "Son, I'm going to hand the phone to your mother. She can tell you about it better than I can."

I cradled the phone on my chin, waiting for the voice of my mom, trying to predetermine what was going on. I heard her excited voice in the background whispering, "Irvin, why didn't you just tell him?"

He handed the phone to Mom, and she said, "Son, it's your mom. How soon can you come to our house?"

Curiously, I asked, "Mom, what is it you and Dad need?"

"Well, a burglar broke down the sliding glass door in the dark, early this morning," she anxiously replied.

With my pulse increasing, I inquired, "What? Are you and Dad okay?"

"Yes, we're fine! A great big angel ran him off and the police have already arrested him," she reported, quite pleased with her story.

Confusion mixed with intense concern stopped me from wanting more details. "Mother, I will be there in forty-five minutes. If you need anything before I arrive, you can call my cell phone."

Hanging up the phone, I rolled over and attempted to explain to Barbara after she'd asked, "What was that all about?"

"Odd as it may sound, Mom and Dad were rescued during a home invasion by their guardian angel. Mom always taught me everyone has an angel assigned to us to protect us in times of trouble."

Barbara rolled over, looking out the window as the morning rays danced across the window sill, saying, "This I am sure of! They've come to our rescue more than once!" Sliding her feet onto the cold floor, she pressed me to hurry. "I'll make the coffee. You can drink it on your way."

The steaming cup of coffee helped soften the bite of the cold blustery wind blowing the leaves across the driveway. As I sat there waiting for the engine to warm, the aroma of fresh coffee filled the chilly vehicle. Backing down the driveway, warmed by a hot cup of coffee and pleasant thoughts, I began my short journey across the city to see about my aged mom and dad, remembering the stories mom had told me about the voice of God and how she had heard from Him on many occasions. Now they had been rescued by their guardian angel, who seemed to always show up throughout the years when trouble was close by. This was incredible!

Arriving at their small frame house, I walked around to the rear of the home where Dad had just finished covering the

sliding glass portion of the door with plywood to keep the
blustery wind from blowing in. Putting his tools away, he
turned to grab me with a big bear hug as together we made
our way through another door into their humble yet inviting
home. Mom was already cooking her famous double chocolate
pie and all the broken glass had been swept and placed in a
cardboard box nearby.

As I kissed the side of her face, she excitedly asked me to sit
down. "I want to tell you the whole story." With her sea-blue
eyes dancing, she said, "I'm going to tell the story my way! Last
night was different from all the rest! One day you can retell the
story because you know how, better than Irvin or me."

Dad realized this was no dream but a real, living nightmare.
No more prompting was necessary. As he had sat up in bed
to calm his terrified wife, he heard the sounds of breaking
glass. Reaching for a claw hammer he had hidden beneath
his bed for emergencies just like this, he struggled to his feet,
stumbling in the dark, and crashing into the closed bedroom
door. Frantically searching for the door knob, he finally found
it. Turning it quietly in his sweaty palm so not to alert the
intruder, he slipped through the bedroom door and down the
hallway. He lumbered with his trusty weapon in hand perched
high, beside his right ear. He was ready to take on any and all
intruders—man or beast. This time they had broken into the
wrong house!

As he came into the dark family room at the back of the
house, he heard footsteps behind him. Instantly, he whirled
around to face whom he thought would be the enemy, but
instead it was my ninety-eight-pound mother in her soft, white
cotton night gown with pink flowers scattered on a field of
roses. In her right hand she clasped her weapon of choice—her

old, tried and proven sword she had used to conquer and vanquish every foe.

With her long, thin, bony fingers she pressed it close to her heart—her old, worn King James Bible that lay on the nightstand close by her bed. Mom looked straight at Dad and assuredly said, "Everything will be all right. Jesus is here with his guardian angels to protect us."

Dad turned around and edged closer to the end of the hall. They could hear the sounds of howling as they entered the family room. His face met a blast of wintry wind coming through the crushed sliding glass door.

As the two old warriors stood there, Dad with his claw hammer gripped tightly in his right hand and Mom holding her old weathered Bible to her heart, they looked at the floor.

Propelled across the room and covering Dad's favorite chair, where he had spent endless days dozing and snoring or possibly ignoring my mother's continual stories about heaven and hell, was crushed glass, shredded pieces that glistened almost like diamonds scattered across the aqua blue linoleum floor.

Whoever entered had broken the glass door down using a large rock that lay nearby. A sense of peace came over them as they thought the night burglar had disappeared. *Who is it? Someone is knocking on the front door.*

Dad's anxiety increased instantly, and heat prickled his underarms, his chest, and back. With his false teeth grinding and every muscle tense and the hammer still raised in his right hand, which had begun to shake with the anticipation of the possibility that the burglar now was knocking at the front door. A voice came through the loose window panes of the old, cracked, wooden door. "It's the Fort Worth police department. Open up!"

Dad was not about to fall for this prank. Knowing what he would do now, he carefully but quickly unlocked the door with his left hand on the doorknob and the hammer in his right hand, ready to slam it into the head of the knocker. Softly, Mom reached out and placed her hand on his and said, "Irvin, it's okay. I called 9-1-1 before I left the bedroom."

Dad took a deep breath and exhaled, opening the door. They were greeted by a police officer who identified himself as Officer Wiley. Why was he smiling? His countenance held a look of amazement. I'm sure it was not every day he received a call at 1:30 in the morning to be greeted by a half-bald, white-headed old man standing there in his blue-and-white striped underwear with a claw hammer in his hand, with a white-haired woman in her nightgown clutching an old Bible against her heart standing beside him.

Without further delay, Officer Wiley asked to see where the crime had taken place. He walked down the hall to the family room, stepping carefully through the broken glass scattered everywhere. He bent down to pick up the large rock used to break down the glass door. Sitting down with Mom and Dad to write his report, he informed them that the suspect was already apprehended and safely in his custody in the back seat of his squad car.

Dad spoke up. "What do you mean, you have already caught him?"

The officer replied, "As I was on my way to your house, a man ran out into the road a few blocks from here, waving wildly for me to stop. I pulled over to see what this frantic man wanted. His terrified pleas were, 'Help me, help me! There's a great, big man in white, eight or nine feet tall with big feathery wings on his back, chasing me!' He begged me to arrest him, saying he had broken down a sliding glass door to steal an old man's television so he could sell it for drugs."

Officer Wiley finished his report, assuring them this would be the last time he would need them because of the suspect's arrest and confession.

Closing his notepad, still smiling, he said, "I have been on the police force for fifteen years and have never had anyone stop me and ask me to arrest him because a big, white angel was chasing him. Before tonight, I never believed in angels and I was not certain there was even a God! But this was before 1:00 this morning. When I am finished with my shift, I am going to pray to this God Who came to your rescue and ask Him to come into my heart."

With a smile of amazement still on his face, he left, waving good-bye, and drove off into the night with his happily shackled passenger.

Voices, visions, and yes, even angels seemed to be my mother's frequent companions. As Mother finished her fascinating story, it was clear to the three of us that God had performed another miracle that enabled us to have this time of celebration.

It had been a few weeks since I had been to their house and Dad decided to take advantage of my being there to get my help with a repair project. "Son, do you have time to help me pull the commode?" he asked. "I can't seem to stop it from leaking."

"Let's go look at it," I said.

As I entered the door of their only bathroom, I tripped over the orchid and green linoleum that was curling up from the floor. Kneeling close to the white porcelain commode, I could see the problem.

"Dad, the base is cracked."

"I know, Son. I tried to tighten the bolts to stop it from leaking. That's when it broke," he confessed.

Dad and I spent the remainder of the day replacing the commode and installing new flooring.

Finishing the repairs, I was confident Mom and Dad were safe and in angelic hands. I hastened to leave, smiling warmly. I hugged Dad and kissed Mom good-bye.

Noticing the sun, a massive red ball of fire, melting into the Texas horizon, meant I would be driving home in the dark. Within twenty minutes I settled in behind the long line of cars with their headlights on, moving at a snail's pace into the darkness. Thinking of the exhilarating memory of the large, white celestial being with feathery wings brought to my mind another intervention of the mighty hand of God as He sent His angels on assignment to save the innocent life of my twelve-year-old-daughter, Taleesa.

Early one Friday morning her frightened voice echoed down the hallway into our bedroom. Jolted out of my slumber, sitting up in bed and shaking the cobwebs from my mind, I yelled, "Taleesa, are you okay?"

My heart slowed a beat as I waited breathlessly for a reply. Hearing nothing, I jumped out of bed and ran down the long hallway, glancing through the open door of her bedroom, seeing nothing. I ran frantically to the doorway of the large sunken den. I came to an abrupt stop, frozen in position so I wouldn't take even one more step into the flooded room. My heart froze as my mouth dropped open, seeing my beloved daughter standing transfixed in water that completely covered her ankles only inches away from an electric floor plug gurgling with smoke rising from the water.

"Taleesa, baby, don't take even one more step!"

In wonderment, she turned and looked at me with those big brown eyes, her bottom lip quivering, and asked, "Daddy what happened?"

That's when it hit me! I felt a genuine, unexplainable peace cover me. Peace! The very concept seemed ludicrous under such circumstances. The water should have been completely electrified, bringing instant death to my unknowing innocent daughter.

Sensing the presence of holy angels in the flooded room, I moved without reluctance, throwing away all caution. Reaching her quickly, I lifted Taleesa up into my strong arms and carried her to safety in the higher elevation of the kitchen nearby. Unafraid, I trudged back through the water, warning the rest of the family of the perilous situation.

Shielded from anxiety by a steady calm, I re-entered the smoking, gurgling waters to gain access to the source of a large broken water line that feeds through an electric hot water heater, in the higher elevated family room. With water blasting me in the face, I struggled but was able to reach the red handle to cut off the flow of gushing waters.

Soaking wet and hardly able to see, I moved on to the electric breaker box to cut off the electricity to the floor plugs in the den. Returning once again to what should have been a watery death chamber for our daughter, I stood with Barbara in awe of the amazing God Who had shielded and protected all of us from harm.

Within two hours a master electrician arrived in response to my phone call. His first stop was the electrical panel box to make certain I had thrown the correct breaker. Satisfied, he came into the elevated family room, stopping short of the steps that descended into the waters, afraid to take another step. His shuddering words were, "All of you should have been killed when you stepped into the water!"

The evidence continued to mount. Undoubtedly, the angels of the Lord entered the waters with our sweetheart daughter, saving and preserving her life!

Five nights later at 2:30 in the morning, in the darkness a loud knock resonated down the hallway, jolting me out of my deep slumber. Sitting up in bed and attempting to gather my senses, I heard Barbara whispering, "What was that noise?"

Softly pressing my fingers to her lips, I said, "Shhh, lay still; I will be right back!" Moving quickly down the hall, looking first into the nearest doorway to my left, Taleesa's bedroom, I saw her sleeping peacefully. Satisfied, I took four giant steps to the next door on my right, peering inside of the dimly lit room. There sat my middle daughter, Tamara, with eyes wide open, staring straight at me.

Without moving her head, she spoke with trembling lips, "Daddy, there's someone knocking on my window!"

I instinctively wanted to crash through the window to put an end to the intentions of the potential intruder. Instead, I walked gently to the side of her bed, pressed softly on her shoulders and snuggling the covers around her, saying, "Sweetheart, lay still. Daddy will find out who it is and be right back."

Kissing her on the cheek, I turned and glared with vengeance at the window where the knock had originated. Moving swiftly in a dead run, reaching the master bedroom and jerking the closet door open, I reached high onto the top shelf for my hidden magnum pistol I had purchased for such occasions as this. As my fingertips touched the cold steel chamber of the powerful pistol, securing it in my clenched right hand, for a moment I experienced exhilaration racing through my veins.

Then I heard a voice speak the old familiar refrain, "Peace, be still." Calmness settled over me like a cool, gentle rain on a hot summer day. Then the faithful voice whispered astonishing words in my ear that caught me off guard. "Alan, don't be afraid. There are more with us than there are with them." Instantly, my eyes were opened. I realized that lurking around the outside of our rural home were not humans, but fallen angels of the darkness, powers and principalities of this dark world.

I reached high upon the shelf, replacing the revolver carefully into its hidden compartment. Then I moved contentedly through the bedroom and out the back door. Taking a deep breath, exhaling as I walked fearlessly into the darkened front yard, I could only see a small post lamp shining dimly, casting eerie shadows throughout the densely wooded acreage, creating an atmosphere of strangeness. I stood transfixed, my eyes searching intently for earthly or spiritual beings. Suddenly I heard sounds of rustling wings. *Or was it leaves blowing in the stillness of the night?*

As I looked up into the towering oak trees, not even one leaf was moving. My face beamed brighter than the lonely post light as I stood in amazement at the greatness of our God, Who created all things that are created yet remains mindful of His dependent mortals.

Walking on air, I re-entered our incredibly secure home, stopping first in Tamara's bedroom. I found her already peacefully asleep, wearing a smile on her angelic face. Kissing her softly as not to awaken her, I returned to the side of my darling wife, who now only needed reassurance that all was well!

> When the servant of the man of God got up and
> went out early the next morning, an army with
> horses and chariots had surrounded the city. "Oh,

my lord, what shall we do?" the servant asked. "Don't be afraid," the prophet answered. "Those who are with us are more than those who are with them." And Elisha prayed, "O, Lord, open his eyes so he may see." Then the Lord opened the servant's eyes, and he looked and saw the hills full of horses and chariots of fire all around Elisha.

—2 Kings 6:15–17 NIV

CHAPTER 15

TAKEN HOSTAGE

I received a shocking phone call that shook my world to its very foundation. The call came from my sister, Sue, who had followed in my mother's footsteps into the medical field to become a registered nurse.

With a quivering voice, she was hardly able to speak these words, "Alan, you and I must have a private talk tonight. I'm here in town and will remain for two or three days. Can we meet at the old café not far from Mother's house for dinner?"

I was hesitant and said, "Sue, it isn't out of my way to come by Mom and Dad's to pick you up." Sue was extremely secretive about our meeting. We closed our call as I agreed to come by at 6:30 that evening. I couldn't imagine what this must be about.

As I pulled into Mom and Dad's driveway, much to my surprise, she was standing on the front porch waiting for me. As she stepped into my Chevy Suburban, Sue noticed my inquisitive look. "It's okay. I told Dad you and I were going to dinner and I would wait for you on the front porch."

As we entered the restaurant, a young hostess met us, politely telling us we could seat ourselves wherever we pleased. After we ordered our food, I looked at my sister and asked, "What does this meeting consist of and why is it so hush-hush?"

Sue took a deep breath and said, "Alan, I hardly know how to begin. I want you to know I have been monitoring mother for a number of weeks now. Have you noticed Mom has a serious problem?"

I interrupted, asking, "What kind of serious problem are you speaking about?"

"Mother's memory is deteriorating fast. Last week when I came into town, I took her to Dr. Chapman, her family doctor, and he is very concerned. He said Mom needs to see a neurologist."

A neurologist? Her words jolted me! I knew I had been extremely busy as the founder and pastor of a growing church named Father's House. I had also continued to design and build Mediterranean homes in the renowned areas of Colleyville and Southlake near Ft. Worth. My demanding schedule filled every waking minute of my day.

Our waitress interrupted us with our food order. My appetite had suddenly disappeared. Sue continued, "Mother has full-blown dementia."

I blurted out, "What do you mean, she has dementia?"

"It's the beginning of Alzheimer's, a degenerative brain disease that will gradually rob Mother of her memories and the ability to care for herself. Alan," her voice softened, "it eventually will kill her."

Sickened, I shook my head and said, "Sue, you can't be right. Are you certain of this diagnosis?" My disbelief diminished as she shared details I hadn't noticed.

"Mother's memory is slipping so fast, it is becoming dangerous for her and Dad to live alone. Today she didn't notice that the pilot light failed to light the burner on the stove. After turning it on high, she left the kitchen and walked outside into the backyard to rake non-existing leaves.

"I smelled a strong natural gas odor coming from the kitchen. The gas fumes filled the whole room. Immediately, I located the unlit burner that was on and quickly turned it off. I grabbed Dad by the arm and took him outside to the backyard, leaving the sliding glass door open for fresh air to blow in.

"When Mom saw us, she laid down her rake and started toward the open door. I grabbed her to prevent her from entering the house. Mom pulled away from me and rudely asked, 'Who do you think you are giving me orders?' She didn't even recognize me."

The pain of the undeniable truth Sue shared with me sunk in. I saw it.

Little by agonizing little, my mother lost more of her memory. She did not let it go without a fight. Her angry refusal for assisted care caused me to take protective measures for her and Dad. I turned the gas off at the wall of the kitchen cooking stove. Dad would have to become a gourmet microwave chef.

Every Sunday morning a group of volunteers picked up Mom and Dad and took them to the church where I pastored. Mom's memory diminished to such a degree that she hardly knew any of my daughters, their husbands, or her great-grandchildren. One Sunday morning Mom stood out among the entire crowd. Not only had she dressed in her Sunday best, Mom had on three complete dresses and the top layer was on backwards.

Barbara, not wanting Mom to be a spectacle, took her by the hand and walked her into the ladies' room. Gently and lovingly, she removed the top two layers of clothing. Mother was amused at how Barbara had noticed her extra dresses.

Barbara commented laughingly, "I understand how difficult it must be to decide which one to wear between such pretty dresses."

"So you have the same problem I have," Mom musingly replied.

Barbara smiled, placed her arm around her, and together they walked back into the sanctuary where the worship was already under way.

That afternoon I sat alone, not wanting to face reality. I allowed my mind to carry me back in time to the stories my mother told me of how she wanted me to remember her.

It all began in a small country town, Morgan, Texas, where a young married woman walked down an old dusty road on a late summer night. Drawn to an open-air camp meeting with slatted wood benches and sawdust covering the parched ground, she was intrigued by the sounds of old gospel songs ringing out into the darkness, accompanied by guitar and accordion music. The singing had begun, so she slipped into the second row from the back.

Thinking no one would notice her, she was amazed when an elderly lady, wearing a full, ankle-length dress, turned and walked to the row where she sat. She greeted her with a sweet smile and handed her an old song book. Turning to page ninety-three, she found the words strange, something about an old rugged cross. Everyone, all fifteen of them, stood with tears streaming down their faces, softly singing with their hands extended toward the heavens.

When the songs were finally all sung, the preacher walked to the old podium and thanked everyone for their faithful attendance. He acknowledged her as a visitor, and reminded them, "Be sure to greet her after church."

My young mother had never met such friendly people before. She listened closely as the old brush-arbor preacher told the story of a Christ Who had died on Mount Calvary to give Himself as a ransom for lost humanity. At the close of his message he asked if anyone would like to come forward to repent and be saved from their sins. Deeply moved in her heart, with tears streaming down her face, she went forward and knelt in the sawdust at an old wooden altar and gave her heart away to the One named Jesus, Who had died for her.

Her friendship with Jesus would flourish and grow into an everlasting relationship that would carry her through every life journey she experienced. Mom told everyone that her love for Jesus grew sweeter as the days went by.

My mom never met a stranger. She always wore a warm smile and carried a twinkle in her sea-blue eyes. It seemed to me she loved everyone and always made herself available to help those in need. Her life was fulfilled by gathering up clothes, canned goods, or old pots and pans to take to a needy family at least one Saturday every month. Regularly, she made me go to my toy box and pick one toy to give to a little boy who did not have any. I hated the very thought of giving up my beloved toys to anyone, until I did it. The joy it brought to the dirty-faced little boy with a torn shirt and holes in his jeans, who clutched it to his chest, holding it proudly as if he would never let it go, taught me God's principle of "better to give than to receive!"

Mom was so proud she was able to be the only high school graduate from a poor family of six children. She reminded me that she had graduated as valedictorian of her school and whispered, "Don't tell anyone, but there were only twelve."

Her studious pursuits led her into the Word of God. Her ability to read and memorize the Scriptures amazed me. She could quote most any scripture in the Bible, with its chapter and verse, and it astonished many of her students whom she taught in her adult men and women's Bible study groups. For thirty-eight years, she taught and shared with zeal and excitement her love of Jesus Christ. To me, she was truly a saint, teaching me more about godly living than anyone else.

Mom was not content with being at home, raising three children, teaching Sunday school classes, and keeping after Dad. Feeling the need to help others more, one day she decided to return to school—nursing school. She dove into her studies of human anatomy and its related sicknesses and diseases, loving every minute of her classes. After one year, she proudly graduated at the top of her class, which in itself was amazing because she was ten to twelve years older than her classmates. Once again, she credited her success to her unique memory.

Mom entered a new dimension, one she called her mission field. She walked the third-floor, east-wing halls of Ft. Worth Harris Hospital, entering the catacombs of the sick and dying. In those days the terminally ill were placed there to live out their last days. This floor had never seen a human being who burst forth with so much love and compassion as she carried out her medical duties with a high level of professionalism. But it was her divine duty and she felt her responsibility to go the extra mile to soothe a fevered brow with a cold cloth and ask if she could pray for the patient. Many times she was there to see a person take their last breath and comfort the families with the blessed hope of life after death.

Her patients and their family members began to see her much like Mother Teresa, who gave her life for those impoverished, without food or adequate medicine, starving, and dying on the streets of Calcutta.

A large group of witnesses called my mother an angel sent to help those in need with words of encouragement and a willingness to go the extra mile for others. I am among those who believe that, just as Mother Teresa was a saint, my mother was a saint, too.

Showing no mercy, Alzheimer's took Mother hostage. I was left with no alternative but to make a most difficult telephone call to my brother-in-law, Bernie Thompson, a trusted friend of mine and the husband of my sister, Sue. Bernie was revered by his many long-time friends, me included, as a man's man, full of courage and fortitude to make the right decisions in the face of great difficulty. Today would be no exception.

His quick and unselfish response was to move Mom and Dad to Mexia, Texas, so they could be close to them. They would provide a beautifully refurbished frame home for them on nearby acreage on their ranch. They could live there as long as possible. This would give Dad a feeling of independence and Sue could be there to check in on them.

Bernie and Sue lovingly took on their shoulders the large responsibility of caring for our aged father and our mother who had fallen victim to the most hated thief that had robbed her of the memory she had cherished.

Long weeks and months passed with great difficulties for them both. The cooking, housekeeping, laundry, and continual oversight of Mom and Dad soon became a twenty-four hour a day endeavor. Bernie and Sue's quality of life was swallowed by the never-ending demands of those whose health and minds had been taken prisoner by this unrelenting disease.

Sue's health began to fail her and Bernie struggled physically himself. Reaching the place of total exhaustion, they realized it was impossible to continue this great sacrifice and labor of love.

Mom and Dad came to stay with Barbara and me for thirty days until we could find a place for them in a local nursing facility. The days with them were most enlightening, as I looked deep into the darkened caverns of Alzheimer's. I saw the excruciating pain on the faces of loved ones forgotten by Mom.

One day our electricity was shut off because the bill had not been paid. I wondered, *What could have happened to the bill? Why wasn't it paid?*

Two weeks later, Barbara found the stack of unopened mail that Mom had hidden in the back of a closet. She seemed to wander aimlessly, looking for something she could not find or something she had lost.

Food was of no interest to Mom, who acted like she did not know what it was. Still, we gathered for the evening meal with Mom and Dad. One evening we had a dinner to remember! I hope it never fades from my memory. Barbara and I saw for the first time the benefits of Alzheimer's.

Mom turned and looked at Barbara, saying, "I don't know who you are, but you certainly are nice." Then, smiling, she looked at me, whom she still recognized, and said, "Son, me and this old man sitting over there have never had a cross word."

Tenderly, I looked at my mom's smiling face, as the twinkle in her blue eyes had returned for a brief moment. Then I looked at my dad, who let out a joyful response, saying, "That's right, Irene." He smiled and winked at me because he and I both knew in all those sixty years, Mom and Dad had had many skirmishes. She had called me to their house on various occasions to be the peacemaker between them.

Joy flowed from the depths of me, knowing Mom no longer remembered the pains of yesterday. But greater still, she no longer harbored in her mind the horrifying night her beloved son was murdered in cold blood. If forgiveness is freedom, then forgetting is liberty!

Too soon, we had to do the unthinkable—place both of them into a nursing home in the Ft. Worth area. Their stay in the home was abbreviated when Mom was rushed to a local hospital after falling and breaking her hip.

Disturbed, Barbara and I rushed to North Hills Hospital within forty-five minutes of notification of the emergency. The wait was more than an hour before the door of the waiting room finally opened. A tall, distinguished physician of about fifty walked in, asking if the Youngbloods were present.

We quickly identified ourselves and, after a brief handshake, he explained to us that the X-rays had revealed a major decayed arthritic hip. He explained that patients' hips break and then they fall. This was his assumption about my mother's accident, and then the first bombshell dropped into our bunker.

The operation was scheduled the following morning, but he explained, "It will be impossible to repair. The only alternative would be to lock the hips into place, and this will render your mom unable to ever walk again."

The waves of the sea had become angry and our small vessel was tossing about violently. Nausea came into my stomach as the thought my mother, who had loved to walk the halls of hospitals caring for others and who loved to walk the aisles of her beloved church greeting people—would never do it again. I remembered her sitting in the second row of our church, singing with her lovely voice praises to her wonderful Lord and Savior, Jesus Christ. Never again would she see her son, her favorite preacher, step to the platform, move to the pulpit, and break the Bread of Life.

It was over! Although Mother was alive, it was as if she had died. This was more than I could accept. The following morning, the orthopedic surgeon took on the task of repairing and immobilizing my mom's severely decayed hip. The operation presented its own challenges. Arthritis had taken a greater toll than the doctors had anticipated. She would survive to live another day, but the verdict was final. She would never walk again.

The decision to lock Mother's hip in place loomed large in my mind, but it would pale in the light of the meeting two days later. I met with the same physician again. I found he was not only was an excellent doctor, but also an extremely sensitive person.

We had lunch in the hospital cafeteria. There he told me of the most agonizing decision he had ever made in his life. With tears in his eyes, he told me of his love for his mother, who had also suffered with Alzheimer's. We shared similar stories, laughing at a few memories, but mostly we reminisced about our loved ones, which brought great sadness and the feeling of loneliness for the days we cherished before this devastating disease appeared.

Finally, he was able to reveal the real purpose for this discussion. He gave me a medical thumbprint of the degenerative character of this hated disease. Once it steals the memory from one's brain, nothing is left but waste areas that will never be restored again. What is lost will be lost forever!

He explained further, "All that is left are the memories you can cherish of your beloved mother and how she once was."

Troubled, I interrupted him, "What is the most difficult decision you have ever made?"

Reluctantly, he began again, "Your mother is where all Alzheimer's patients eventually reach."

Sensing his deep concern, I asked, "Where are you going with this?"

He struggled again and said, "All Alzheimer's patients lose their ability to eat. The most loving and merciful decision I had to make was to deny my mother food by a feeding tube. She died less than ten days later."

Emotions erupted out of me like a spewing volcano. I struggled to keep my food down. Anger, rage, and confusion consumed me. *Could he be insinuating I should deny my beloved mother food and watch her starve to death?* I looked at him in disbelief and abruptly told him, "I'm not ready to make this decision yet!"

I immediately made it clear that he should order the feeding tube for my mom. Quickly, unable to control my emotions any longer, I thanked him, left the cafeteria, and walked outside of the hospital. A fresh, westerly breeze blew in my face and it was just beginning to rain. This was a welcome moment because it could conceal the tears streaming down my face.

Life hadn't prepared me for this devastating decision of whether to deny my mother life-sustaining food for her body. Everything within me screamed, *How could I ever eat again, knowing my mom was starving?* My heart still aches today on behalf of those who are forced to make such drastic decisions for their loved ones out of moral and logical necessity.

Denial, despair, even confusion swirled in my head. I felt as if I were walking in a dark, heavy fog. Circumstances beyond my control were forcing me to make dreaded and hated decisions that left me with the feeling of guilt and worst of all, the feeling I had failed my mother and father at the pinnacle when they needed me the most. I had come short of being the man they believed I was!

After seven days Mom was released from the hospital. Usually this would be a time of celebration, but not this time. Hospitals have their own odors, which are not offensive. Their patients are young, middle aged, and elderly, with the majority recovering to go home and eventually to enjoy life once again.

But I knew a truth deep in my heart—my mother would never go home again! On the contrary, she would return to the catacombs of the dying, seemingly without any hope. Among hollow eyes and speechless mouths, where emptiness reigns and loneliness rules, she would go back to the nursing home and its rank smells of body waste and urine, with yelling and cursing and crying from those who could speak. Even louder than all their voices was the "silence" of those who could not.

It was two days after Mother returned to the "house of horrors" before I made my appearance to visit my mom. Saturday morning in the darkness I was awakened by the voice of God instructing me as to what I must do. Once again it required my obedience to His voice.

CHAPTER 16

ALZHEIMER'S BOWS ITS KNEE

I jumped out of bed and stood, anticipating this day. I had already had my wake-up call and my instructions. Today I wanted to awaken the dawn, armed with the Word of God empowering me with His authority, ready to deliver a barrage against my hated enemy, Alzheimer's. I was confident that through faith, the Word of God coming from my mouth would bring even Alzheimer's trembling to its knees.

Enough is enough! I refused to sit idle any longer without taking action. This day would be remembered in heaven and in hell, when Alzheimer's bowed its knee to the Living God and the Lamb!

Walking over to the side of the bed where my beloved wife slept, I gently shook her until she woke up. Pressing my lips against her ear, I whispered, "Sweetheart, it's time to get up." She turned over on her back, stretched, and lifted her head, looking around in the semi-darkness. "Why so early?" she questioned.

I informed her of my instructions. In the military they're considered marching orders—direction I had received before dawn from God Himself concerning the surprise attack against the thief called Alzheimer's that held my mother's mind in his cold, dark sway.

As the sun rose, it sent its light rays across the city. Ft. Worth would have a visitation from heaven. Even the dew drops glistened with anticipation as we arrived at the nursing home shortly after 8:00 A.M. I could smell the sweet aroma of the presence of the Living God and His angels. I did not see them, but I felt them. If you listened closely, you could hear them all around the room. They had come, not to observe, but to witness the power of the spoken Word of God.

Barbara and I marched in side by side, holding hands and swinging our arms between us joyfully. I stationed Barbara outside as a sentry to guard the door, to prevent passage by anyone until I returned from within the room where Mom and Dad lay in separate beds a little more than ten feet apart.

I stopped first at Dad's bedside. When he saw me smiling, he spoke, "Hello, son. Your mama seems to be asleep. Are you going to wake her?"

I looked at my dear old Dad and leaned over close to him, patting him on the side of his face, looking into his blue-gray eyes. "Dad, I'm going to wake her from the sickness of her mind so she will know all of us again."

Dad broke down and began to cry. Through his quivering lips, he said, "Do it, son!"

I turned and walked across the room to my mother's side. I reached down and gently shook her, speaking to her in a soft voice. "Mother I am here." With those crystal blue eyes, she turned to me with a questioning look, like, "Wow, who are you?" I bent over and kissed her on the forehead. "Mom, it's your baby boy, Alan Dee. I am going to tell you something you may not know. You are a victim of Alzheimer's. It has stolen your ability to talk and recognize your family. I believe that because of what I'm about to do, you will recognize your family and talk to us once again.

"Mother, don't become nervous or frightened as I pray for you. There is nothing for you to do. I will do it all, just hold my hand."

I remembered that in the darkness of the morning and in the presence of the Holy Spirit, I had made my decision. No longer would I cower to this hideous disease, which had run amok in my mother's mind for far too long. My resolve was to expose and bombard it with the power of the Word of God, which I was confident would cause it to release its hostage.

I began to pray, "Alzheimer's, His name is Jesus. Before Him every knee will bow and every tongue will confess that Jesus Christ is Lord. The Word says whatsoever you bind on earth will be bound in heaven. In the name of Jesus Christ of Nazareth, I bind up Alzheimer's by the authority and power of the Living God! Mother, let this mind be in you which was in Christ Jesus" (Phil. 2:5).

Forcefully, I prayed with faith, believing, "His Word says the things I loose on earth will be loosed in heaven" (Matt. 16:19 NIV). "Mother, I loose your mind, your memory, and your tongue to speak again. Alzheimer's, you let her go! You no longer have dominion over her. Bow your knee, you despicable disease, and confess Jesus Christ is Lord!"

I opened my eyes and looked down at my precious mother. Tears streamed freely down her sunken cheeks, a smile caressing her lovely face. I reached for the pink box of tissues nearby, removing enough to wipe away both of our tears. Across the room, I could hear my dear old dad blowing his nose.

Then looking into her eyes, I said, "Mother, I love you." With her precious head nodding, I knew she was saying "I love you, too!"

As I turned to leave, I said, "Mother, soon you will know who I am once again." At the door, I took one last glance at Mom and Dad. Barbara had waited faithfully at the door on the other side. Closing it behind me, I heard her say softly, "Honey, do you know how loud you were?"

Smiling, I said, "You mean you could hear me?"

She nodded her head and said, "They heard you down the halls and all the way to the nurse's station. The head nurse came by with a concerned look on her face and asked if everything was okay. I assured her, explaining my husband was praying for his mom."

Barbara and I left just as we had entered, holding hands, confident we had been obedient to God, and we knew without a doubt that He would do the rest.

Sunday morning dawned bright and beautiful. The birds were singing and joy and thanksgiving abounded in our hearts. I decided to share with the congregation of Father's House, where I served as senior pastor, about the miracle I was certain would reveal itself in the near future.

Before the message, I shared what had taken place at the nursing home on Saturday, so all who heard my voice would be witnesses of the power of God against the stalking disease called Alzheimer's. I told the story of Jacob when he wrestled with God, saying, "I will not let you go unless you bless me."

The one he wrestled with asked him, "What is your name?"

"Jacob," he answered.

Then the man said, "Your name will no longer be Jacob, but Israel, because you have struggled with God and with men and have overcome" (Gen. 32:26–28 NIV).

I told the people the only path to victory, whether it be setting young men and women free from drugs or obtaining healing for our minds, souls, and bodies, was to identify the enemy, call it by name and use the Word of God against it, fervently and effectively applying it by faith and releasing it into the hands of God, remaining confident that He will complete the work that needs to be done. He is the Alpha and Omega, the author and finisher of our faith!

Then I revealed to them how I had wrestled with God in the darkness of the previous morning, asking Him to bless me by restoring my mother's memory.

Confident in the Living God, I said, "I cannot release my mother to die until she is able to recall her loved ones and speak their names once again. Only then will I submit my will to release my mom into Your loving arms, so You can take her home to be with You forever."

The following days were days of expectancy. I thought any time something good was going to happen. Before long, the days became weeks, and I'm sure the doubters multiplied. The voice of the adversary heckled me in my mind, saying, *What a fool you are. Your mother is going to die, and what will you tell the people?* Viciously, I resisted these voices that taunted me in my head, not allowing them to discourage me.

The long weeks became months, and still I refused to surrender to Alzheimer's and my hated adversary, the devil. Holding tightly to the promises and trusting in God to fulfill His Word, I was confident He would not fail me.

Then on a glorious Thursday, a phone call came on my cell phone I will never forget. I heard my sister's trembling voice, and my heart sank as her words came slowly. I took a deep breath, for a moment fearing the worst.

The last thing I expected to hear was my sister questioning me. "What have you done to Momma?"

"What do you mean, what have I done to Momma?"

In between the sobs, I heard her say, "When I walked into her room today, she turned her head and looked straight at me with those sea-blue eyes. She smiled and called me by my name. Alan," she reminded me, "Mom hasn't recognized me as her daughter or called me by name for more than a year."

Sue lived in a distant city and I had not made her aware of the declaration and the battle waged to recover our mom from the grasp of the hands of the dark one, the devil, who is out to steal, kill, and destroy any and all who will not wage war against him.

Our phone call was brief, allowing Sue to get back to our mother. This was a moment she thought was gone forever. Turning my truck around, I headed home to announce the good news to Barbara in person. "Alzheimer's is bowing its knee."

With jubilation, I called our youngest daughter, Tricia, who was away at a university in Houston. Trying not to give away the surprise, I simply reminded her to be sure to come home that weekend.

Worried, her first words were, "Is everything okay with Grandma?"

I calmly responded, "She is doing fine."

Tricia always stopped by the nursing facility to see her grandma on her way home. She usually stayed for an hour or so, carrying on a one-sided conversation without any response or acknowledgment. She always left saddened, crying and brokenhearted.

We both expressed our love and said our good-byes over the phone. She had to get back to her studies.

It was three weeks before Christmas almost to the day when, seventeen years before, the uninvited guest had entered by truck and pressed me to "ask God to reveal Himself to me." God's revelation of Who He is through His love for humanity and His unmerited favor to all who seek Him continues to amaze me in every way, even to this day!

Tricia arrived, road weary, late Friday afternoon. She walked down the long hall to her grandma's room methodically, expecting nothing unusual. As she entered, her grandma turned her head and shoulders to gaze at her youngest granddaughter as if there had never been a time of Alzheimer's captivity and calmly said, "Hi, Tricia."

Lovingly, Mom reached over and patted the bed with her left hand, motioning Tricia to sit down close to her. Tricia's mouth opened, gasping for breath. This could not be real. She must be dreaming! Walking in shock, she made her way to the bedside and sat on the edge of the bed. Looking deep into those blue eyes, she saw the look of one no longer "absent." It became a laughing and crying celebration. Grandma was awake from her sleep!

The following Sunday I announced to the expectant witnesses at Father's House Church that Alzheimer's had bowed its knee and Mother's mind had awakened from its long sleep. The celebration was rowdy and boisterous as praise to the mighty God filled the air. At last, our turn came that afternoon after lunch, when Barbara and I walked into Mom's room. How could I ever forget her angelic face? Walking across the room to her bedside, I kissed her on the cheek.

Her first words to us will ring out forever into eternity, never to be forgotten, "Son, is there still faith out there?" That's my momma!

I laughed until I cried and answered, "Yes, Momma, there are still those who have faith in God and always will."

Barbara took her by the hand and she called her by name. She then turned her head and looked at me, questioning, "Son, are you still preaching the gospel?"

Smiling through the tears, I said, "Yes, Mom, even today we celebrated the liberating power of our God and the healing virtues that still flow from the sacrifices of His Son."

I had never anticipated Christmas so much. During the next two weeks, all but two of the family members made their way to the bedside of Grandma. Only our sons-in-law, Mark and Greg, couldn't arrive until Christmas Day. The tree we had placed in Mom's room on top of her dresser was adorned with lights, tinsel, and colorful balls of all different shapes. Gifts from all were wrapped and placed beneath its branches.

Momma was in a smiling, festive mood this Christmas Day, and her eyes twinkled as she heard us coming down the hall, singing, "Joy to the world, the Lord is come, let earth receive her King." Gathering beside her bed, we broke into singing her favorite Christmas carol, "Silent night, holy night, all is calm, all is bright."

Each one handed her a gift. Mother opened them with Tricia's assistance and enjoyed every moment of the celebration. Mom had already recognized Greg, but one family member was left. Halfway through the last gift she was opening, lying there in her bed with all of her granddaughters, their husbands, and their children gathered around her, she looked intently at Mark, who was standing at the foot of her bed.

She gazed admiringly at him and said, "There's my pretty boy, Mark."

The room went silent. Tears flowed freely. Mom recognized her last family member present. She had called *all* of us by name!

I slipped out the door into the hallway with tears streaming down my face. I had to do what should have been the most difficult decision I could ever make. The last time I was faced with this decision of surrendering to her death, I could not make it, but this time I could!

The covenant was made and God faithfully had delivered the blessing. Now I had to let my mom go. My words were hardly audible, "Thank You, God. She's Yours; You can have her."

The next four weeks flew so quickly! Mom developed pneumonia and gradually slipped away into the regions of semiconsciousness.

There she lay, Momma, a ninety-eight pound legendary woman with all of the qualities of a hero. She was a stalwart in life with outstanding spiritual strength.

Throughout her entire life, whether in storm or rough seas, she did not waver.

Few have witnessed such tenacity on this earth. Her persistence in maintaining her grip with her mind, body, and soul, and holding to her faith—the substance of things hoped for, yet the evidence of things unseen—never failed her.

The epic battle between Momma and the last great enemy, death, would always remain as a legacy to those who follow. Her final act of heroism fulfilled her high calling in Jesus Christ. It staggered even her formidable enemy, whom she fought gallantly to the very end.

My darling mother always had a saying, especially when things were tough. She would whisper in my ear, "Be a good soldier, fight the good fight, never surrender, and always remember; we're the Youngbloods."

Early in the morning before 5:00 on January 20, 1998, the holy angels came and carried her away to her eternal home. I can only imagine that in front of the crowd gathered to welcome her just inside the gates of pearl, were Dad, who had arrived just four months before, Dennis, her handsome, blue-eyed son, and of course, baby Charlotte, her angelic granddaughter. They didn't need a formal introduction. She already knew them and once again called them by their names.

Three days later, as I stood at her funeral, my last words belonged to her—they were her legacy:

> For I am already poured out like a drink offering, and the time has come for my departure. I have fought a good fight, I have kept the Faith. Now, there is in store for me the Crown of righteousness, Which the Lord, the righteous Judge, Will award me on that day—And not only to me, but also to all those that long for his appearing.
>
> —2 Timothy 4:6–8 NIV

This story is lovingly dedicated to the families and the thirty-five million people worldwide who live with Alzheimer's disease or other types of dementia. May it restore hope and guidance to you on behalf of your loved ones.

CHAPTER 17

THE JOURNEY

The piercing sound of my pager going off interrupted my busy work day. As I reached to silence its high-pitched beeps, my eyes locked upon its messaging window. I saw the universal code for emergency, 911, flash three times. Quickly, I rushed to my automobile to retrieve my cell phone to call my wife. We had established by an earlier decision that this code would be used only in *extreme* emergency situations!

With high anxiety I dialed her number, trying not to panic. I realized panic on my part would affect my emotions and my ability to think and respond with the wisdom I needed in times like these. *Who, what,* and *where* screamed into my ear as her cell phone rang three times before she answered it. Finally, I heard her voice! It was subdued—she was unable to conceal her terror as it leaked out from the corners of her mouth. With hushed tones she urged me to come as quickly as I possibly could to North Hills Hospital, some forty-five minutes away, where our youngest daughter, Tricia, struggled between life and death. Pressing me to hurry, she ended the conversation, unable to discuss any further details.

I was already in my truck, driving with my emergency lights blinking. Sliding frantically onto the freeway, drivers yielded, allowing me to maneuver in and out of traffic. My mind traveled back some thirty years to a situation very similar to the one I believed we were facing now. I will always remember that day!

While at a construction site in another city, a police officer had rushed up, sliding to a stop, startling all of my employees. As he stepped out of his patrol car and walked hurriedly toward me, I recognized him as a friend, which brought a small sense of relief.

The closer he got the better I could see the solemn look in his eyes, which increased my anxiety about what could have caused his sudden and abrupt arrival. My eyes searched his facial expressions as I tried to determine the reason he was here. His cordial greeting could not hide the seriousness of the look on his face, and I knew something was terribly wrong.

"Alan, it's Barbara," he began.

Barbara was seven months pregnant. He let me know she had been rushed to the hospital and had given birth to our second child—"Baby Charlotte."

He was still speaking as I jumped into my car immediately. No matter what words he chose—he could never soften the blow; our baby's life was in peril. Frantically, I drove as fast as possible, but I was too late! Baby Charlotte died, leaving me without the opportunity to even say, "Good-bye."

I was jolted back to my own present time and space with the sound of a loud air horn from an eighteen-wheel truck breaking into the nightmare of my memory. That's when terror gripped my heart, attempting to take my mind hostage, telling me the same tragedy I experienced before was about to repeat itself.

I determined in my heart it would not. Knowing this time exactly what to do, I recalled how the psalmist David called upon the Lord in his time of distress and so did I. My urgent request was directly to God. I desperately asked Him to send a guardian angel to stand watch over my daughter's life until I could get to her side.

Finally, I arrived at North Hills Hospital. I pulled into the parking lot, jumped out, and ran as quickly as I could into the surgical waiting area, looking frantically for a familiar face. Then I saw my wife, Barbara, and son-in-law, Jay, sitting with solemn expressions on their faces. Walking briskly through the crowded waiting room, I reached Jay's side before he saw me.

His first words were, "Daddy, I'm so glad you are here."

Hugging him close, I asked, "Is Tricia still in surgery?"

He looked at me with big sad eyes as he spoke softly. "We haven't seen anyone since they took her into the operating room."

Jay was the newest member of our close-knit family. What a blessing to have him join us on this journey of life with our youngest daughter, Tricia. Instantly, his personality won the hearts of every single one of us. The excitement he wears around his head is like a halo that warms the heart of everyone around him.

Shortly, the door to the operating room opened and a tall, blonde surgeon, pulling his mask down below his chin, stepped toward us. He motioned for Jay to come closer to him.

Jay, with his long wavy hair flying all about his head, was out of his seat in a flash. He reached the side of the tired-eyed doctor, placing his left hand on his shoulder. The last audible words I heard came from Jay's strong voice tenderly asking, "How did the surgery go? Is Tricia going to be all right?"

The tone of the physician's voice was soft, almost muffled. He spoke very few words, none of which Barbara or I could hear, but the look of concern was unmistakably imprinted on his unshaven face. Turning to his left, he pointed to a long hallway nearby and disappeared through the doors he had entered moments before.

Jay turned toward us, making a gesture that partly covered his mouth, and whispered loudly, "Come on, Mama, come on, Daddy!" He turned quickly, motioning with his right hand for us to follow him. He moved rapidly down the hallway with us following, trying to catch up with him.

Arriving ahead of us, Jay pushed open the door to the small private family waiting room. He reached over and hugged us, saying, "I love you, Mama," wiping a tear from his eyes. I looked deep into his eyes, trying to read the inaudible message the physician had shared with him just minutes before. Pulling me close, he looked into my eyes and said, "I love you, Daddy."

I turned and looked at the private room that held only eight chairs pressed closely around the room, realizing there was not enough seating for our entire family. To a degree, I was relieved . . . the rest of the family had not arrived yet. Fighting the anxiety of not knowing the status of Tricia's condition, I remained quiet. So did Jay and Barbara.

The quietness was finally broken when the surgeon in charge came in behind us and closed the door. He was sensitive and addressed us in a personal manner. Encouraging us to identify our family connections to Tricia, he shared some of the details of the lengthy surgery.

"I have just witnessed the worst sight my eyes have ever seen in my seventeen years of surgery," he said. In layman's terms, inside Tricia's abdomen he found that the smooth, transparent membrane that lines the cavity of the stomach was massively infected and inflamed by peritonitis. The staph infection was so extensive that everything infected had to be removed—specifically, two sections of her small intestine including her appendix. The deadly infection had covered the entire lining of the abdomen, including all of her reproductive organs. It had been spreading for eighteen days from the perforated small intestine leaking bodily waste fluids into the cavity of the abdomen, causing extreme damage.

All of this was a result of a minor outpatient procedure that went bad! Jay and Tricia had just returned from their honeymoon in Europe. Tricia had previously made an appointment with a different physician, who had diagnosed the condition as endometriosis. The corrective operative procedure was performed with a laser during microscopic surgery. Unknowingly, the small intestine was damaged when the laser burned small holes into it. This critical mistake brought our entire family to the crossroads of our journey and the new bride and bridegroom to a four-way stop sign.

Sitting there, I sensed that each of us was dazed by the physician's post-operative comments. The three of us posed our questions of concern for Tricia. Barbara, knowing her daughter's mothering intentions, spoke hesitantly, "Will she still be able to have children?"

Not waiting for any further questions, the chief surgical physician stood up and looked intently at each of us. Breathless, we waited for his reply. With the most serious expression, he said, "The question of having children is not what you should be concerned about. Most importantly, Tricia is alive!"

He excused himself and turned to leave the room. I slid up close to him and whispered in his ear, "What is my daughter's condition?"

Gravely, he replied, "Extremely critical—her life is hanging by a thread!"

I was not expecting this response and immediately I asked him, "Where is she?"

He spoke without reluctance. "Tricia is in a private recovery room further down the hall, past the elevators on your left. A trained specialized nurse, who will not leave her side until her condition improves, is personally attending her. I've done all I can do!"

I looked at him, questioning, "Can I go be with her now?"

Looking slowly for a moment at each of us, he responded, "Only one at a time can be in there. By all means, don't get in the way of her attending caretaker."

These were his last words. He turned and walked away, leaving the door ajar. Jay, knowing me well, understood without my asking. He said, "You go first, Daddy. See about Tricia. I will follow you later. Right now, I'll stay here with Mama until the rest of the family arrives."

I left the waiting room, trying not to run, hurrying past the elevator to the nearest door on the left. Standing close by was the tall, blonde physician. Politely, he gave me entrance into the locked door.

As I entered the room, I was astonished at the sight of Tricia's emaciated, ninety-eight pound body connected to every conceivable life support apparatus imaginable, but I refused to allow what I saw to overwhelm me. When I entered the room, I heard a still, small voice say, "She will live and not die!" I could sense the atmosphere of warfare! The struggle for life against death was in full force.

I introduced myself to the highly skilled medical assistant who was moving methodically from one machine to another as she monitored each reading with precision. I moved cautiously, getting close to Tricia's bedside, and leaned over the small rail to kiss her white, ashen forehead. I whispered to her, "Daddy is here. I will not leave your side until you are safe!"

As I raised my head, I noticed a small monitor blinking with large red numbers. Sensing it was sending a message of great importance, I slipped over to the medical attendant and asked her about the function and importance of this particular device. She explained, pointing to a specific monitor, saying, "The number, fifty-two, is Tricia's heart rate." Her voice softened. "Thirty minutes ago her blood pressure fell to the point we almost lost her."

Anger rose up in me against the enemy who had come to steal my daughter. I joined the battle, fighting alongside the guardian angel I knew was warring at her side. Together, we could defy death, who had come to take her life!

Defying him openly, I said, "Death, I'm speaking to you in the name of Jesus! I demand you remove your hand from Tricia's life and let her go!"

The intense struggle lasted for more than an hour, but little by little the monitor began to report the message—the tide of battle was turning. The strategy of our warfare was prevailing over sickness and death. No longer could I hold back my jubilation, as I sensed victory was certain. I began to rejoice, whispering close to her ear the ancient truth that always rules, "At the name of Jesus, every knee will bow and every tongue will confess Jesus Christ is Lord!" A smile of relief came over the wonderful assistant's face and she said, "All the monitors are giving an 'all safe' reading."

Her condition was upgraded to serious, allowing her to be moved to a private room. When you walked into her room, if you weren't prepared to see the shocking sight of a young woman whose body had been drastically altered by a medical blunder, it could take your breath away. With large tubes going in and out of her stomach and every type of tube or wire conceivable dangling from her thin, frail arms, your mind could play tricks on you, wondering if it was a human or a wooden marionette doll with jointed limbs that move by manipulation of its strings and wires.

The long days and nights she lay in the rest stop gave opportunity for others to come and pray, led by mighty warriors, Marcus and Joni Lamb, who stopped by with prayers that helped bring healing to her mind, body, and soul. Announcing the prayer request on television allowed thousands to join with us on this journey, helping us to realize we were not alone.

At this juncture, the spiritual and physical life merged together on her journey. She soon learned that the outcome of this crisis would make the decisive difference in her life's travels. This "detour" became the turning point, leading her on a different trail than she had ever walked before. I can say, with experience, it's a scary, narrow path that leads us down into steep, rocky canyons and through dry, desert places where dangers lurk behind every dark shadow. We are all witnesses because she has brought her family members along with her on her journey.

In our spiritual travels, though weary, we began to climb higher and higher. Constantly, we felt His big, strong arms picking us up and carrying us to the top of the mountain, where our joy and laughter echoed down through the valleys we had just passed through. His presence was always with us, causing us to realize we were not alone but escorted by God and His mighty angels!

We stopped long enough to take a deep breath of fresh mountain air, and then we noticed an old wooden cross with a sign attached by nails, pointing down the path we had just completed. The letters, though faded with time, were written in crimson red. The name of the path revealed its origin and its ancient author who named this path "Trust." Though it proved very difficult, we were learning to place our confidence for life's trials and the outcome into His hands.

After forty-two days in the hospital, with her husband always by her side, Jay and Tricia's dream to be parents began to fade. Slowly surrendering to a body damaged by a deadly infection and scarred by the knife of the surgeon who fought to save her life, and worst of all being marred, mentally and emotionally in her own eyes, it seemed her ability to have children was gone!

Feeling desperate, she turned to a fertility doctor, a superb Asian specialist. He discovered through extensive tests that her fallopian tubes were damaged and suggested a procedure identified as IVF, in-vitro fertilization. After two attempts, Tricia slid into the depths of despair, realizing she would never carry a baby. To her it was a dream lost; her dream of motherhood had been stolen. She grieved as if a child within her had died.

Needing a place of refuge, she eventually returned to the church where she was a vocalist. One Sunday as she was singing, a vision of a large angel with beautiful wings appeared. He walked up to her and, from his strong arms, handed her a precious newborn baby. She realized this baby was a gift from God!

Like a warm blanket, the vision spread hope over her emotions. As the church service ended, she hurried to her mother to share the good news God had shown her. With tears of joy flooding down her face, she blurted out, "Mother, when I was singing on the platform this morning, God gave me a vision of an angel bringing me a newborn baby. I looked and instantly I knew the baby was mine, but what was strange was that I realized I had not given birth to it. I have always believed I would be healed and be able to have my own children, but this did not seem to be the case."

Standing there somewhat bewildered, Barbara placed her arm around her shoulder and said, "Tricia, maybe God is going to provide a surrogate for you and Jay." Quickly, her eyes opened with enlightenment and her heart was prepared for a baby, in whatever manner it would be birthed. She took a deep breath, saying, "I'm ready now to have a baby however God wants to give it to me."

With renewed excitement, she returned to the fertility physician and informed him she was willing to walk any path necessary to become a mother. Then he asked her, "Do you have a sister?" Joyfully, she responded, "I have two sisters. One has already volunteered to be my surrogate! Yesterday I called my sister, Tamara, and shared with her the vision and told her I needed a surrogate."

Tamara's enthusiastic outburst told it all when she instantly replied, "That's the least I can do for you, my sister. Nine months of carrying a child for you is nothing compared to my lifetime on earth!"

Tamara reached down her hand with arms no longer crippled to pick up her sister who had fallen into despair on the difficult road of life. Hope and excitement were restored in Tricia's heart.

Running ahead of us with exuberance, she continued her journey to such an extent she almost ran past a sign that read,

"Yield." Confused, she stopped and looked, wondering where the main thoroughfare was. All she could see was a narrow entrance to a steep rocky path. Stopping for a moment, she heard the voice of her fellow Traveler asking tenderly, "Will you give your baby back to me?"

Fear gripping her heart in agony, she cried out in pain, "The task You ask of me is too great! I cannot surrender my plans, my will, and my life completely to You; this sacrifice is more than I can bear!"

She was overwhelmed by this acknowledgment. She continued her journey with tears blinding her vision. She failed to see the old weathered road sign at the narrow entrance leading up the steep rocky road, written in crimson red. It was marked *Surrender!*

The transfer of the frozen embryos into Tamara's body was successful. Everything was coming together for my two daughters on their way to fulfilling Tricia's dream. But the first negative pregnancy test proved equally devastating to both sisters. It seemed as if an earthquake had ripped a giant crevice across their path. Not just one of them, but both had lost a baby!

Tricia, heartbroken, returned to the fork in the road—the one with the sign marked *Surrender*. There, through great difficulty and with tears flooding her eyes, she released everything completely to His control. The outcome of the journey ahead belonged solely to Him!

The fellow Traveler lifted both women's heads and wiped the tears from their eyes, enabling them to try again. I can still hear their unbending determination as they declared, "We will do it again and again until we birth a child together." So they did.

I can still hear the echoes of their laughter as if it was only yesterday when my two daughters birthed together Jay and

Tricia's first son—Justice Blaze Jenson on February 4, 2003. His miraculous birth brought a spontaneous tribute from Tricia's heart on behalf of her sister, whom she has immortalized as a saint, honoring her with these words:

> You—my sister—came to me in my darkest hour.
> You were not afraid to enter into the darkness with
>   me.
> You walked in and brought the comfort of God,
> You were able to hear hidden fear in my voice which
>   no one else could hear.
> You saw sadness on my face no one else saw,
>   even when I tried to hide my worry or pain.
> You saw straight through me.
> You, Tamara, were trusted with the most precious
>   aspect of my life.
> You were like an angel sent to earth for me.
> I can never thank you enough!

Don't forget his name—Justice Blaze Jenson! One day this child will grow up to be a leader and a trailblazer for others!

The journey continued, taking many side roads. It had carried Tricia into places she had never been before. Each stop and every detour had a purpose—to reveal the fellow Traveler who had walked every step of their journey. He had traveled this way many times before.

I can still hear our three daughters as we traveled on vacations across the United States. Their sweet voices echo in my ears with the old, familiar refrain, "Are we almost there, Daddy?" One more mountain, just one more valley, a few more tears, and a lot more laughter!

It had been four joyful years since Justice Blaze was born. That's when Barbara and I realized there was something going on. The two sisters were whispering, sending secret e-mails, and making private cell phone calls to each other. They thought they had us fooled! But we knew they were at it again. The sisters finally revealed that they were going to try to have another baby!

Surprise! Surprise! This time it will be easy! Nothing to it! The Asian doctor has it down now! Tamara took all the necessary shots to prepare her body for the successful transfer of the embryos. Tricia put on her full battle gear, standing fully surrendered to God, trusting Him wholeheartedly. His ways and plans are perfect, she has learned. Now she tells me, "Don't leave on life's journey without Him!"

All was well! The procedure was flawless and successful. They were on their way again! Then disaster struck like a tornado from a clear, blue sky! Tamara gathered herself and made the most difficult call she had ever had to make. She had miscarried; the baby died. And with it the dream of the two sisters perished forever . . . lost in their ocean of tears!

Tamara was crushed and Tricia was devastated. Tricia wanted to be alone. She was grievously wounded, mad, and frustrated. She knew Who had the answer, and she would never stop until she got it. Tricia heard Him say, "You will find me when you seek me with all your heart" (Jer. 29:13).

She went after Him, pursuing Him night and day. She assailed Him, saying, "I've done everything you asked of me. I've surrendered all; walked in obedience; stood on your words, unwavering. I've not doubted, neither have I given up. What more can I do?"

Reaching the end of herself, she sobbed. She felt His strong arms surround her from behind as He picked her up, His tears streaming down the side of her face. He shared her pain and sorrow, lifting them from her and placing them upon His shoulders. At last they were one.

Rejuvenated, the two sisters were at it again! They said this would be the last time. *Sure, we'll see!* I thought.

They returned to the same doctor and went through the same familiar preparations. Emotionally drained but excited, the two sisters and their greatest cheerleader, their mother, arrived at the medical office complex. The realization that today would be the final attempt to implant the last of the living embryos weighed heavy on them. Nervously waiting in the lobby for the elevator, Tricia tried to control her breathing to hide her anxiety.

Looking at her older sister, she asked, "Are you okay, Tamara?"

Turning toward the open lobby, her eyelashes battling away the tears of grave concern over her body's readiness, she was relieved when she heard the soft bell signaling the elevator's arrival. Slipping through its open doors, she smiled and replied faintly, "I certainly hope so!"

In silence they exited the elevator and walked the short distance to the medical office of the fertility specialist. Upon entering, they were greeted by the upbeat receptionist. "Well, ladies, this is the big day we've been waiting for. Is everyone ready?"

Gathering themselves and putting on their best smiles to conceal their nervous apprehension, the three ladies in faith replied, "We're ready!"

At this gesture, the attendant led the women to separate examination rooms. Stopping at a nearby room, she asked Barbara and Tricia to wait there while she took Tamara down the hall to another room. Tamara followed her down the long hallway to a private room where she would wait for the doctor.

She walked over to the examination table, which was covered with a soft white pad. Taking off her clothes and brown leather sandals, she slipped into the gown that was provided and lifted herself onto the bed. Lying there, she drifted into the comforting memories of giving birth to four healthy children. Having babies had become second nature to her.

Her meditations were interrupted by the doctor's familiar voice. "Good morning, Tamara."

Jolted from her thoughts, she opened her eyes and replied, "Good morning, doctor." Holding her file in his hands, flipping the pages, he commented, "Before we implant the last of the embryos, I am going to do one more sonogram just to make certain we're ready."

Feeling better from her meditations, without batting an eye she responded, "Sounds good to me!"

The nurse prepared her for the sonogram. The skilled physician with his trained eye looked intently at the condition of the uterine lining. Finishing the procedure, he looked at Tamara, troubled, and said, "Tamara, I'm sorry. I don't know why, but the lining did not respond properly to the medication. It is not thick enough for the embryos."

Her heart sank. Hot tears began to fall like a late summer rain. With her throat dry, she asked with a pleading voice, "What do we do now?"

The kind physician patted her on the hand, nodding his head, and replied, "The only hope we have left is to implant the embryos into Tricia."

The summer rain exploded into a full-blown thunderstorm, washing away the doctor's remaining remarks. As she sobbed uncontrollably, she pulled on her clothes and slipped into her sandals. The nurse, who had walked the length of this journey with them, began to cry also.

With one more valley, one more mountain to climb, she started down the long hallway with the nurse holding onto her, to inform Tricia of the heartbreaking news.

Finally, she arrived at the room where her sister was waiting. Had she stopped and looked above the door, she might have seen an old familiar sign written in crimson red. The letters, though faded with time, read, "Trust."

Entering the room where her baby sister and mother were waiting, not able to break the news eloquently, Tamara blurted out, "It's all up to you now!"

Shocked and stunned by her sobbing sister's words, Tricia turned and said, "What . . . what do you mean?"

At this moment the doctor stepped past Tamara into the room. Speaking with a soft, assuring voice he said, "Tricia, Tamara's not ready! You are the last chance for the remaining embryos to survive. Let's do a sonogram to just see if it is possible for you to be the one for us to place these embryos into!"

Surprise! Surprise! The sonogram revealed the hidden secret. God had restored her female reproductive organs! The extensive damage from staph infections and severe scarring from four operations had been restored to such a degree that the fertility specialist felt confident Tricia could carry and bear her own children.

Instead of Tamara becoming pregnant, it would be Tricia!

The next nine months offered challenges, but they were nothing this journey had not prepared Tricia for. Her confidence in God and full reliance upon His Word carried her safely to the birthing place God had prepared.

The dream became reality! Tricia successfully gave birth to her second son on March 26, 2007! She named him appropriately Journey Zade Jenson, who now joins our grateful family in our earthly travels here below.

Our journey of life together will carry us up one more mountain and down one last valley, as our fellow Traveler leads us safely to our final destination, where He, the Lord God Almighty, reigns in His new heavens and new earth! There, waiting patiently for us, will be our heroes who have crossed over death's valley and landed safely in His strong arms. I can almost see her now, "baby Charlotte," a young lady, beautiful and vibrant with her face all aglow, running to meet us with her arms outstretched to join her beloved family, never to be separated again!

> "Trust in the Lord with all your heart and lean not on your own understanding. In all your ways acknowledge him, and he will direct your paths."
> —Proverbs 3:5–6 NKJV

CHAPTER 18

THE BANNERS

Barbara drove carefully onto the church's frozen parking lot that was covered with a thin sheet of glistening ice. Veering to her left, she brought the silver-gray SUV to a sliding stop just inches from the blue and silver sign with the reflective symbol of a wheelchair on it.

With my hands firmly braced against the gray padded dash, I turned and asked her, "Do you realize this is a handicapped space?" Without batting an eye Barbara replied sweetly, "Well, don't you think this is appropriate? After all, you are on crutches."

I reached abruptly across my body with my left hand and opened the door on the passenger side, trying to conceal my frustration. Carefully, I slid the aluminum crutches under my armpits, placing the weight of my body on my left foot. I turned cautiously around on the slick, crunchy ice, leaning over to look at her through the open door.

Treacherously, I negotiated my way across the icy surface. Finally reaching the double glass doors that led into the church, I was thankful to find them held open by an associate, David, who looked at me, stunned, and asked, "What happened?"

I grimaced and shifted my weight onto my left leg, as David reached down to touch my badly swollen foot. "Your foot is twice the size of normal. It looks like it's about to burst and it is burning up with fever."

Straightening up, he questioned me, "Have you been to a doctor?" The conversation I desperately hoped to avoid now required full disclosure.

"David, I fell on the ice playing a game of broomball with our youth and cracked my collarbone last Saturday. On Monday morning I woke up and this is the way my right foot looked. So yesterday, I went to a podiatrist to determine what was going on. After a thorough examination he determined the problem was not in my foot. Instead it was somewhere near my shoulder blade and would require outpatient exploratory surgery, which is scheduled for Friday morning."

Then I leaned toward him as best I could on my crutches and whispered my secret to him, "By Friday, I believe I will be healed and will cancel the operation."

With a weak smile, he said, "Your first cancellation may be the service tonight. The forecast calls for more sleet and rain, ending after midnight."

David was right. We lingered around the church for a short while and then returned safely to our home.

Upon exiting our SUV, Barbara helped me into the kitchen. I went to the pantry and reached for the can of Folgers® coffee. She looked at me and said, "What are you doing?"

Now was the time to let her know just how determined I really was. "I want you to go upstairs and go on to bed. I'm going to stay up, read my Bible, and seek God for divine intervention on behalf of my injuries."

She looked at me wearily, rubbed the back of her neck, and asked, "Do you want me to stay up with you?"

There never was a moment I didn't want her by my side, but tonight would be long and difficult. I preferred she get a good night's rest. Supporting myself on one crutch, I leaned over and kissed her goodnight, prompting her to go upstairs to our bedroom and go to sleep. Reluctantly, she did.

Once she disappeared down the hallway and up the stairs, I returned to the kitchen to finish making a pot of fresh coffee, feeling certain I would need every drop to make it through the long night ahead. As the coffee pot began to perk, quickly I slipped the crutches under my arms and made my way into the family room.

It took a lot of extra effort, but I finally reached the CD player. I loaded it with a selection of my favorite praise and worship songs, especially those that clearly exalt the Lord our God. With music filling every corner of the room, I turned off all the lights except one lamp that I allowed to remain burning dimly on a table at the end of the brown leather sofa.

Singing the words of the song playing softly, I poured my coffee and returned to the family room and began to praise Him. The more I praise Him, the larger He grows in the eyes of my faith, until He looms like the mighty Warrior He is, Who always brings victory and conquest against every foe. This night was no different.

I laid my crutches aside, raised my hands to my Maker, and walked around the room, doing my best to ignore the excruciating pain. I declared God's greatness by quoting scripture after scripture, knowing every promise was mine if I could grab hold of them by faith. I knew God would intervene in my behalf!

Unable to take another step on my badly swollen foot that was in unbearable pain, I stopped walking but refused to surrender, standing with the majority of my weight on my left foot with full determination to secure healing in my body. I was surprised to hear the voice of my Redeemer in the early hours of the morning. He spoke softly. "You are an army, terrible with banners."

His words stunned me. Through my tears, I questioned, "What did You say?"

"Alan, you are an army, terrible with banners."

I had never heard this terminology before. I wondered what it meant. And I asked Him, "What does this statement mean?"

Instantly, my mind went back to the days of Israel when Joshua led them. As they marched from conquest to conquest with the banners hoisted high, they displayed their victories against the fallen kingdoms one after another, striking terror in the hearts of their enemies. God always fought for Israel.

Then pictures began to play on the screen of my memory from the war manuals I studied, of fighter planes returning to their bases with banners emblazoned on their fuselage of the enemy planes they had shot down or destroyed. Then the pictures changed to warships returning to port from the theater of war in places such as the South Pacific in World War II. Banners flew from ropes attached to the mighty masts of ships they had sunk in naval battles and the war planes they had knocked out of the sky and sent flaming to a watery grave.

I watched in my mind as the scenes of warfare changed from the distant hills of Judea to the gray, threatening skies of

Normandy. They faded as fast as an enemy's war plane burning without wings, plunging into the depths of the South Pacific.

The presence of Jehovah-Nissi, Who is the "Lord our Banner," illuminated the eyes of my understanding, showing me marching with a mighty army of believers with banners unfurled, displaying above our heads the many victories obtained in time of trouble or sickness. These battles were furiously waged in the "trenches of faith" and the "bunkers of trust" until at last the believers were able to charge up the mountains of impossibility, planting the flag of their commander-in-chief, Jehovah. They laid claim to all He has promised and provided through His Son, Jesus.

Awestruck and overwhelmed, I walked gingerly across the room to the big, brown sofa chair, easing myself down gently into its soft, warm cushions. I lifted my feet and slid them on top of the footstool. Looking up, I noticed sun rays dancing across the windowsills, peeking through the wooden blinds, announcing the dawning of a new day. I crossed my ankles and my eyes fell immediately upon my right foot, which was the same size as the left!

Startled, I uncrossed my feet and shoved the footstool out of the way. I hurried across the room and switched on the overhead lights. Standing in amazement, I looked down again. It was impossible to determine which foot had been enormously swollen and burning with fever. Both were normal, with high arches and long, thin toes and sharp defined ankles protruding from either side of my feet. The pain was gone!

Perfect—picture perfect—just like new, as if nothing had ever happened! Picking up my Bible, I searched and found the scripture, "You are beautiful, O my love, as Tarizah, comely as

Jerusalem, terrible as an army with banners" (Song of Sol. 6:4 KJV).

Thirty minutes later, the coffee perking, canned biscuits buttered and baking, Barbara arrived in the kitchen, asking, "How did it go?"

I looked down and said, "You decide."

Her eyes followed mine intently and then with astonishment, she inquired, "Which foot was swollen?"

She raised her brown, loving eyes from the sight of the amazing miracle back to mine, blinking away the tears, and whispered, "Do you know how much I love and admire you?"

Her words did not catch me by surprise. Reaching tenderly to smooth away her falling tears, I wrapped my arms around her, pressed my face to hers, and clung to her as she clung to me. Clearing my throat from the hoarseness of battle, finally able to respond, I said, "Early this morning in the darkness, but in the revealing light of His presence, I reviewed each and every miracle you and I have ever been given. Thankfully, I counted all the blessings I have received. They are immense, yet there is one standing out above them all."

Hesitating, I laced my weather-beaten fingers through her flaxen brown hair and smiled, "Do you know which one it is?"

Her eyes blurred, looking deep into mine. "Which one?" she asked innocently.

Tightening my long, lean arms around her body, I lifted her feet off the floor, swung her from side to side, and confessed over and over, "You! You! You are the greatest blessing I have or will ever receive from God."

Engulfed in my arms, she beamed back at me, "No, you are!"

Amazingly, we had found each other so many years before and are still hopelessly lost in love. The argument was just beginning as she pressed her finger against my lips, whispering softly, "Do you know what time it is?"

Glancing at the old cuckoo clock hanging on the wall reminded me of a scheduled appointment with a friend. I loosened my grip and her feet touched the floor. Feeling larger than life I blurted out, "While I'm gone, call the doctor's office and cancel the surgery for tomorrow."

Feeling a sinking sensation, she stalled. "What do I tell them?"

Understanding her bewilderment, I nodded. "Keep it simple! They would never understand any way you say it." Grinning, I left in a hurry, knowing she could get to the point quicker than I could.

The months flew by like Canadian geese fleeing the winter cold and buffeted by turbulent winds but still able to rise above and land safely in the warmth of southern sanctuaries. The vision was large. We birthed a church, moved into a wonderful facility, and were busy building and restoring people from all walks of life, teaching and exhibiting faith in the Living God. It was exhilarating and challenging; but more than imaginable pressure crushed us to the point of breaking!

It was as if there had been a secret armistice brokered on our behalf for this season. And it came to an end abruptly at 3:00 on a Sunday morning.

"Je-sus! Je-sus! Je-sus!" The faint cry of His name escaped through the deadly pale lips of my darling wife. Startled awake by her voice, I reached for the lamp on the nightstand nearby. Twisting its switch frantically, in its dim light I could see Barbara's ashen face as she fought for each breath of life. The icy-cold hands of death grabbed her warm, beating heart, crushing it in his vice-like grip. With fatal intentions, he had come into the darkness to steal her life away!

Laboriously, she gasped out words that were hardly audible, "Pray for me." With groans and agonizing moans, she lay grimacing, her face contorted, her body writhing in pain. Horrified and astonished, I pleaded, "What's wrong?"

Words melted into a pot of excruciating pain, leaking out the corners of her parched lips. "I can't breathe!" More gasps . . . moans. "It feels like an elephant is standing on my chest." She struggled to form the words. "It's crushing me . . . pray for me!"

No time to call 9-1-1. They couldn't arrive in time! Coming to my spiritual senses, I called upon the one and only name with all power and authority.

Like a blanket, His presence covered the room with His mantle falling on me. Instantly, great courage and astonishing boldness took over my inner man. I laid my hand on her chest, stared death right in its face, and declared the name of Jesus. I defied death and demanded him to remove his hands and let her go. We struggled and the battle of wills raged. I did not let up and would not until he relinquished his hold on her. I intimidated my hated enemy, reminding him that no longer could he run unabated; all power was given in heaven and earth to the resurrected Christ. "In His authority, you loose her and let her go!"

Minutes passed slowly as we fought. At last, without a choice, death was forced to release his grip; peace flooded our hearts. Her breathing remained laborious as warm colors repainted her face. We snuggled close together with His arms wrapped around us, bringing comfort and assurance knowing He was with us in the room.

Sleep! It was impossible! I lay close, trying to feel her beating heart. Barbara's chest rose and fell sporadically, sometimes in short quick spasms, other times hardly at all. I wondered as I watched the illuminated numbers on the nearby clock, *Was it counting down the end of the life we had so wonderfully shared?*

Dawn crept into the room. Gently, I pulled the sheet over her head to keep the morning light from disturbing her much-needed sleep. My own heart skipped a beat, looking at my beloved with her face covered. I took a deep breath, refusing to believe this was an omen of things to come.

Slowly exhaling, I shuddered. Carefully slipping out of bed with perplexity eating me alive, I staggered, unable to think logically what to do. I thought aloud to God, "If only this was not Sunday morning. There could not be a worse dilemma; how could I make the right decision? Am I not the senior pastor of a growing church, expected to fill my position in the pulpit—a responsible person who believes in keeping commitments? Yet more than these, am I not a devout husband who sees himself as a protector and guardian of those he loves?"

Exasperation ruled in my heart as what to do. Disregarding criticism, I made a heartrending decision. I would take her with me. Sacrificial? Not at all. It only meant helping her get dressed and carrying her into the church. Beneficial? Absolutely; she would never leave my sight!

We arrived on time. As springtime rains showered down, I maneuvered through shallow water puddles, pulling underneath the drive-through carport, sliding to a splashy stop. Opening the car door, we were met by my faithful friend, Brock White. I hurried past him and slid one arm under Barbara's legs and the other around her waist, with her right arm securely around my neck. We entered across the threshold like newlyweds into a long, wide hallway.

Hearing sounds of glorious praise pouring from the auditorium, Barbara exhaled a breath of relief. The people were standing and few would notice as we slipped into the back seats.

Sitting down, I whispered, "I need time to gather my scattered thoughts."

Barbara assured me, "You'll do just fine."

Minutes later, Jim Burgdorf, our worship leader, smiled and nodded his head, signaling me to the front. Wearing a false smile, I reached the platform and my eyes scanned the crowd of friends and loved ones. I realized Barbara and I were surrounded by the greatest people in all the world!

No longer holding back my emotions, I shared the terrifying events of the night and called upon them to carry out the scripture from James 5:14–15: "Is any one of you sick? He should call the elders of the church to pray over him and anoint him with oil in the name of the Lord. And the prayer offered in faith will make the sick person well; the Lord will raise him up" (NIV).

Our courage was bolstered by the corporate prayers of men and women of faith. Among them were battle-tested warriors, fearless in obedience to God's Word, who walked in wisdom and understood God had given incredible knowledge to medical science, enabling them to walk hand in hand to heal sickness and disease.

With Monday morning finally dawning, I made a long, belated phone call to the home of a renowned cardiologist and his wife, whose home we had recently built. Holding my breath until at last she spoke in her familiar voice, I identified myself and she responded, "I knew it was you, Alan."

In explicit details, I recounted the terrifying events of the weekend. When she had heard enough she said, "Alan, what in the world were you thinking? You should have called 9-1-1 immediately!"

Her strong concern numbed me. "Well, I didn't! So what do we do now?"

Anxiously she replied, "Hang up! David's making hospital visits. I'll page him and call you back."

Waiting for her return call, I questioned my sanity. *Had I taken leave of my senses?* Staring at the telephone, willing it to ring, I instantly grabbed it at the first sound, "Yes!"

"David wants Barbara at the clinic immediately! His partner, who lives directly behind you, will be waiting." Sensing my reluctance, she assured me, "Alan, he is a skilled physician. Barbara will be in good hands until David gets there."

Nervously, we entered the cardiologist offices. I commandeered a wheelchair for Barbara, who still was too weak to walk. Within minutes, our neighbor—now our doctor—greeted us. His eyes met mine and I saw his grave concern. He and his nurse wheeled Barbara to the nearest examination room, leaving me alone without her for the first time since the violent episode.

I remained on the edge of my seat, watching the clock on the wall. It didn't seem to move. I continued to take deep breaths, trying to convince myself I had made rational decisions. *Right or wrong, they were mine!* I battled the voice of my accuser—who in my mind called me a fool! Exhaling slowly, I calmed myself as the doctor entered the waiting room.

If a picture can say a thousand words, his face told all! Barbara's condition was desperate! He started, "I believe Barbara has suffered a massive heart attack and possibly damaged the walls of her heart." He looked at me to see if I was taking it all in and continued, "I suggest immediate surgery!"

All the oxygen left the room. My breath was sucked from me. I felt like a boa constrictor had coiled his body around me and squeezed every last drop of life out of me. The mighty man of faith melted to the floor.

I tried to force words to come out of me. I choked, "When will David be here?" Then I saw him. *Thank God!* At this exact moment, Dr. David Carter walked into the room and their eyes met. Without words, the two doctors quickly moved into a private room.

Alone again! The room closed in around me and the boa constrictor returned to finish its job. I slumped into the chair with my eyes wide open—seeing nothing because my ears were bursting with so many voices offering me a melting pot of mass confusion.

David returned alone. With compassion in his eyes, he sat down close to me. "Barbara has suffered a severe heart attack, in my opinion. If we operate, she will not survive the surgery because of her weakened condition."

I tried to stand and staggered to my feet, but stumbled. With tears in my eyes I steadied myself. My heart was breaking! My friend, the fine physician, reached out and touched my shoulder, speaking softly. "Take Barbara home so she can rest and call your daughters . . ." He paused, as if to rearrange his words. Frustration crippled his vocal cords, and for a full minute he couldn't speak.

When he did, all he could say was, "Alan, I'm sorry!"

Inside of me, my faith refused to believe what my ears had just heard. I fought to keep my composure as the specter of death began to gnaw at the edges of my hope.

Unwilling to appear shaken I replied, "David, I appreciate your knowledge and concerns for Barbara. Thank you for your compassion."

Reaching for the car keys, I shrugged. It was a slow, dreary drive back home. I was determined not to be defeated. I sternly told Barbara, "I will not let you die!"

Tears poured from her like a heavy rain. Sobbing, she whispered, "I don't want to leave you alone!"

I looked hard out the window, hoping to conceal my helpless heart. I was the man with a resolve to be strong as steel, yet inside my own fiery furnace, I was melting, not knowing what I would become.

We reached the house. Lifting her into my arms, I carried her to the bedroom, tucked her in, and kissed her tenderly. "I will be in the next room making some phone calls. If you need me, let out a little yell and I will come running," I whispered.

She nodded.

It was difficult to adequately convey the feelings of my heart. The grim sentence hung over me like a black funnel cloud. Each call helped dispel the gloom.

Hearing the reports, just like the three Hebrew children our daughters refused to fear the terrifying fiery furnace (Daniel 3). They displayed the same confidence in the God Who delivers us out of all our troubles. Their courage in the face of insurmountable odds could defeat the adversary and make any parent proud.

Finishing my last call, I leaned back and took a deep breath and exhaled a sigh of temporary relief. Within moments the phone rang, startling me back to reality.

"Hello."

"Hey, Buddy, it's Mike. Five minutes ago I learned the news concerning Barbara. Do you want me to come over?" His voice was edgy with expectancy.

I took a moment to ponder the timing of my Jewish friend.

"Mike, Barbara is in serious condition," I blurted.

"I know. That's why I'm calling. Let me do something for you."

Hesitantly, I asked, "Like what?"

"I want to make an appointment for you to see Dr. Feingold, my Jewish doctor. He was Mickey Mantel's personal physician."

"Really!" My heart leaped within me.

Trying to conceal my excitement, I asked him to let me make the appointment, using him as a recommendation. It was as if the sun had burst through the clouds, sending rays of hope through my troubled soul as he consented.

With Barbara's file in front of me, I called the well-known cardiologist who had treated the New York Yankee legend. Mike's name had hit a home run; he would see us right away. With great anticipation we entered his offices, unable to hide our desperation.

His warm greeting soothed my raw conscience. I'm not sure what it was about him, but both of us were enamored by his presence. Relief entered our troubled souls as he meandered through the file. "Alan, you and Barbara get comfortable as I study the reports. My nurse will assist you with anything you need."

Before he left the room, I was compelled to divulge to him, "Doctor, we believe in the Great Physician, Jesus."

Looking back at me firmly, he replied, "I am Jewish. My sentiments are not the same!"

As he left the room, I glanced anxiously at Barbara, who sat silently. She looked at me, glanced at the clock, and sighed. "Why are we here?"

I thought for a moment before answering. "I'm hoping for a different opinion."

How could it be different? Almost on cue, the doctor re-entered the room, staring at the wall behind us. "The EKG indicates you have suffered a heart attack. I agree with Dr. David in his evaluation, not to operate in your present condition. It is unlikely you could survive the surgery."

Sitting in silence, I nodded my head in agreement. As mixed emotions sent a fresh wave of nausea mixed with frustration, I murmured, "Who in the world has the answer?" As we left his office I recalled that my sister-in-law, Joan, had slipped a business card into my pocket three days earlier. She whispered in my ear, "When all else fails, call this doctor, and tell him Barbara is my sister. He and I have been involved with a number of terminal patients. He will work you in quickly."

Despairing but not defeated, I made one last appointment, convinced of finding the answer I desperately needed. Early Thursday morning we arrived at the office of our fourth cardiologist, Dr. Cowden, who became a pioneer in the field of alternative medicine. Upon arrival, we were escorted to an examination room with dull gray walls, a wooden chair, and a small trash can covered with a plastic bag. The nurse handed Barbara the pale-blue, backless gown and directed her to wait on the hard, black leather examination table covered with crackling white paper.

Returning to the room, the nurse surely must have heard my thoughts as they exploded in my head. *My, God, what are we doing here? All we've done is retrace the same path over and over again.* I watched in disdain as she took Barbara's blood pressure and checked for her pulse. The nurse looked up in stunned disbelief and, finding no pulse in the left wrist, she moved quickly to the right wrist, searching. "I think I found one! It is so faint, I'm not sure!"

Looking at Barbara with concern, she flew into the adjoining room. Breathless, she returned with the doctor, who immediately began to search the left wrist for her pulse. I gasped for my breath as I watched his eyes. He did not panic, but fear consumed the room, descending on us like low-hanging clouds, as he failed to find a pulse in the left wrist.

He stopped and looked at Barbara, "Are you feeling all right?"

Overcome with the moment, she whispered, "My left arm is aching."

Smooth and quick, without a word, he listened with his stethoscope, wanting to hear her beating heart. My eyes never left his face. I saw a bewildered smile spread cross his wrinkled face. With his left hand holding Barbara's and his right hand in mine, he spoke softly. "The bad news is Barbara is in extremely critical condition and should be hospitalized. The good news is—I know what to do!"

Speechless, we waited. "I'm going to pray!" He prayed the softest heartfelt prayer I had ever heard. God's peace filled the volume of the room and we left with a rippling sense of elation rising in our hearts. Thankful, Dr. Cowden was a man who prayed for his patients and believed in the power of prayer.

One long, challenging year passed. We lived each day surrounded by His grace and adorned with His mercy. From the very beginning, even before that fateful night, we called upon the name of Jesus. Now we would prove without a doubt the skill of the Great Physician! To accomplish this, we made an appointment to return to the offices of the Jewish doctor. Startled to see Barbara, he blurted, "What are you doing here?"

"Doctor, Barbara is doing very well," I responded.

Taking command, he said, "That's for me to decide!"

"What is it we need to do to prove her heart has healed?" I questioned.

Not lost in translation, he said, "I'm going to admit her by 5:00 P.M. today at Irving Memorial Hospital. Tomorrow morning, I will perform a coronary angiography which will determine the condition of her heart."

At 8:00 A.M., as I stood with a close friend, Kathy, in front of the double doors that led to the surgical room, the cardiologist stepped out with a document and pen in hand. He caught me off guard when he said, "This is a release you must sign. If I find what I think I'm going to find, this gives me permission to immediately perform open-heart surgery."

I hurled back the challenge, "I'll sign it only if you find what I think you are going to find and the credit goes to the Great Physician."

I reached for the document and signed it without any reluctance. He turned toward the operating room and said, "The procedure usually takes forty-five minutes. If I don't return, you will not see me for twelve or fourteen hours."

Believing he would return in forty-five minutes, Kathy and I hurried to the coffee shop. Anxiously, we watched the clock tick off the minutes . . . fifteen . . . twenty, and then at twenty-five the doors opened slowly. His face was white as he stood there in his scrubs. He looked as if he had seen a ghost. I lost my breath, not knowing what to expect.

I walked close to him. "What is the verdict?"

In a daze, he spoke cautiously. "Today I have witnessed with my own eyes *a perfect heart*!"

It was my turn to be stunned!

Then, being a man of his word, he asked, "What is it you want me to do?"

"When Barbara wakes up I want you to tell her exactly what you have told me!"

Like Thomas, the doubting one, Barbara had a compelling need to see and touch the nail scars in His hands, to reach inside His garment and place her fingers on the sacred side which was riven.

Believers search for something—anything—to corroborate their faith. We all want something tangible we can hold onto and say, "Look, world, here is the evidence!"

> Now Thomas, one of the Twelve was not with the disciples, when Jesus came. So the other disciples told him, "We have seen the Lord!" But he said to them, "Unless I see the nail marks in his hands and put my finger where the nails were, and put my hand into his side, I will not believe it." A week later his disciples were in the house again, and Thomas was with them. Though the door was locked, Jesus came and stood among them and said, "Peace, be with you!" Then he said to Thomas, "Put your finger here; see my hands. Reach out your hand and put it into my side. Stop doubting and believe." Thomas said to him, "My Lord and my God!"
>
> —John 20:24–28 NIV

CHAPTER 19

HEAR, O ISRAEL

Never again! Say it again.
Never again! Say it louder.
Never again! Say it with more force,
Say it like you mean it!
Never again!
Say it like your life and others depended on it.
NEVER AGAIN

In 1989, I stood in Jerusalem with pain exploding in my chest, as if a horrific monster had taken his clawed fingers, reached into my body, and snatched my beating heart right out of me. With tears streaming down my face, I experienced a nightmare from hell! To my right, on my left, even above me, desecrated naked skeletons surrounded me. They had been exiled, shamed, and disgraced. Their clothes, including their shoes, were displayed nearby. I noticed a star—the Star of David—hand-sewn on the front of every garment. In the center of the star, the word *Jude* was written in mockery of the heritage they were born with. Everywhere I turned, dead, naked bodies by the tens of thousands lay dumped in open ditches. Thousands stood like helpless mummies, waiting their turn to be murdered by a heartless, demonized maniac, whose father must be Satan himself!

Our guide, a brave and devout Jewish woman, Gia, stood to my left. My wife, Barbara, and I, with our daughter, Tamara, next to us, began our journey into the Holocaust Museum. Before we entered this hallowed sanctuary, we looked up to see a sign. It spoke loud and clear with life commitment and death-defying meaning. Dripping with passion, it screamed with the voices of millions, as if in total defiant determination, those words that ring out boldly: NEVER AGAIN!

Why in God's world was I so visibly shaken, completely overwhelmed with compassion? It was as if my own loved ones had been violated and murdered by an immoral, demonized beast that was hell-bent to destroy us as well. Great passion seized me, with everything inside of me about to explode. I felt my eyes narrow as I gritted my teeth; I boiled with fury and seethed with anger. I was ready to go to war to fight, kill, and destroy the enemies of the Jewish people, whoever they are, who would ever again, through genocide, try to exterminate the "chosen people of God!"

These crimes against humanity must never be forgotten, and those who love Israel must be always on the alert, ready to go to battle to see that this monstrous evil is never repeated.

I tried to reason with myself. *I'm not a Jew.* In 1942, I was born a proud American; the stars and stripes I love. I was honored to serve in the United States military, proud to take the oath to defend our country's freedom even unto death. Every time I hear the "Star Spangled Banner," I become all choked up, tears swell up in my eyes, and once again I am committed to serve, to fight, even unto the death for our freedom we hold so dear. As long as I live, I am committed, totally sold out, with a never-bending will that our flag will always wave over the land of the free and home of the brave!

I have been reborn by the sacrificial blood of the Lamb of God, Jesus Christ. I am a soldier in His army, committed and dedicated to Him and His cause at all times. I am a warrior against the principalities of the dark world, which is ruled by the dragon, Lucifer, the old devil. The enemies of God are now my enemies, whether they derive from man or beast. Those Christ loves, I love, which covers all humanity of the whole earth.

God is angry with those who, through rebellion, have worshiped false gods. He stands against all nations deceived by Lucifer to make war against Jerusalem and Mt. Zion for the evil purpose of inflicting harm or bringing desolation to God's most precious possession, His people, the nation of Israel.

As I pondered these thoughts, trying to come to grips with this outburst of emotion, I began to comprehend exactly what was transpiring. I realized that the enormity of the passion exploding inside of me was not my own, but it was His, the passion of Christ! With great compassion, He wept for all of those who had perished at the hands of the criminals of the Nazi regime. God had not forgotten the horrors of the Holocaust nor the crimes committed against His people, not even for one moment. I could hear Him saying, "Vengeance is Mine, I will repay. Count it all fear to fall into the hands of an angry God."

Still standing outside the museum, pride began to swell up inside of me as I heard the voice of my commander-in-chief. When He speaks all will hear him! What He says will come to pass! The horrors and the hells of the Holocaust, where more than six million precious Jews perished, will *never again* be repeated! The names that ring out in infamy—Treblinka, Auschwitz, and Dachau—will pale in comparison to the slaughter that Christ and His mighty army will rain down on the enemies of Israel in the Valley of Megiddo in the last and final battle, Armageddon. The nations of the world will hear His voice thunder, "NEVER AGAIN!"

I looked at Gia, who had tears in her eyes and had slipped out the back door from the dark room of mirrors, where candles burned in front of each one, accounting for each and every soul who perished in the Holocaust. The reflection of the eternal lights that represent the living memory of the beloved Jews who died was more than she could bear.

I thought I had come to Israel for one solitary purpose. It was not to fall in love with the Jewish nation, and it wasn't necessarily to visit all of the remaining places Christ frequented when He was on the earth. After all, He had died, been resurrected, and ascended to His Father over 2,000 years ago. His own people had rejected Him. They refused to receive Him as their Messiah. Even in Jerusalem today, not much has changed; the mass majority still refuse to acknowledge Him as God, Yeshua or Messiah. So I was certain He had left them alone!

But I was in for a surprise, an awakening of awakenings, to find Him everywhere I went except for one place in all of Israel, and that was the tomb He had once occupied but no longer did because He had risen from the dead!

Our tour, with thirty-eight tourists from the United States, actually began in Galilee. We arrived late one evening with great expectations, even though we were physically exhausted, having traveled by air from Amsterdam to Tel Avi, and then by bus to a hotel by the Sea of Galilee. The sun had set behind the mountains by the time we arrived. It was pitch dark.

For me, the difficulty and the length of the journey were not factors. My sights were set on viewing an extended plain that reaches from the Mediterranean Sea to the northern part of the land of Israel, fifty-five miles north of Jerusalem and only ten miles from Nazareth. The destination I had longed for these past eight years was a place called Armageddon. In the Hebrew, it is called Harmageddon or the "Mount of Megiddo." Har means *mount*, and Megiddo means *slaughter*. The meaning of these two Hebrew words becomes quite clear: Armageddon is the "Mount of Slaughter."

Looking at the clock on the wall of the hotel lobby, I saw that it was already 10:20 P.M. I realized why all of us were so weary. We had traveled since early in the morning and now it was late. Morning would come for us before we were ready for it.

In the darkness I heard a noise in the distance. It sounded like a telephone ringing. *Who in the world could be calling at 6:30 A.M.? Evidently they must not know we are in Israel on vacation.* I rolled over, thinking, *It must be an emergency call from home.*

I reached for the telephone and answered it. The caller's voice had a strong accent. What was she saying? With increased anxiety, I demanded, "Who is this? Oh, okay. Yes, thank you."

Barbara sat up in bed, asking, "What was that all about?"

Somewhat embarrassed, I nonchalantly told her, "It was only the hotel lobby calling for a wake-up call. I must have forgotten I asked for one!"

We jumped out of bed. Time was wasting! This was our first day in Galilee. We dressed quickly. I rushed out the door into the hall to the elevator. By the time Barbara caught up with me, I was holding the elevator door open with my foot.

Breakfast has always been my favorite meal. I looked up at the waitress who had brought water and juice for our table. I explained to her that we were ready to order. She smiled at me and nodded her head as I began to order three eggs, over easy, hash brown potatoes, one thick slice of ham, four crispy pieces of bacon, two buttermilk pancakes, and a cup of steaming hot Folgers® coffee.

She must not have understood what I said because she politely pointed me to the large buffet table in the center of the room and said, "You may serve yourself."

I moved quickly to see what we were having for breakfast; my eyes scanned the length of the table. It was covered with plates of cheese, sliced tomatoes, smoked fish, and all kinds of different breads. *The fish look raw and goat's milk to drink? Where is the Folgers®?* I thought.

Following breakfast we were instructed to gather in the lobby and wait for the arrival of our tour guide. Finally, a fifty-passenger tour bus pulled up and an attractive Jewish woman stepped out.

Walking briskly, she greeted us in the lobby. "My name is Gia. From this time forward I will be your guide. Today we will board a boat and ride across the Sea of Galilee. After a short tour on shore, we will sit for a while on the side of the Mount of Beatitudes where Jesus gave His famous sermons. If any of you would like, you can read the passages from the Bible and experience the sound effects of an amphitheater. Following this, we will walk through the ruins of the fishing village where Simon Peter lived."

With our itinerary explained, we were ready to load onto the first boat and slip on our lifejackets. I remembered that the last boat ride I had heard about on the Sea of Galilee was when Peter, James, and John encountered the fateful storm when Jesus walked on the water.

The large, freshwater lake was calm with our boat filled to capacity. Its passengers had arrived from many nations; their voices were all chattering with excitement as we traveled across the Sea of Galilee. Gia explained how storms can come down between two of the mountains, through the valleys, and across the sea quickly without warning. She informed us that many old fishermen's boats now lay on the lake's floor. They were sunk because of high winds blowing on the stormy seas.

Somewhere in the midst of the roar of the boat's inboard motor and Gia's voice telling us of the history surrounding the Sea of Galilee, I heard a familiar voice saying, "It is I!" Startled, I looked around me. No one was speaking except Gia. Then I took a deep breath and said quietly to myself, "It can't be Him. Why would He be here?"

As far as I could see, there was not a storm in sight and the waters were calm. For a moment my anxiety built and I wondered if there was something about to happen that I was unaware of? *Is this why He is here?*

Then I heard the voice again. It said, "Don't be afraid, it is I."

Quickly, I staggered back to my seat. I had been standing up, looking around. Sitting down, shocked, amazed, and bewildered, I could not comprehend why His presence was here on this boat, on this lake in Galilee.

Stepping onto the shore, Gia pointed to our left, where two or three large round, thick wheels lay. She said, "These are millstones used to crush the olives in days gone by." As she continued to walk and point out various sights and objects, the thoughts in my mind would not leave me alone. I knew Whose voice I heard. It was His voice, the Christ of Calvary, the same One Who walked on the waters of the Sea of Galilee over 2,000 years ago.

My heart raced. I couldn't stand it any longer! In the distance I could see an old, one-story, flat-top building with stairs on the side that led to a rooftop. I quietly slipped away without any explanation to anyone and hurried to the old stairs. Taking two steps at a time, I reached the top rapidly. I walked over to the edge of the roof that overlooked the water and sat down, hanging my legs and dangling my feet over the side.

I was suddenly aware of His presence. He had followed me from the boat, through the crowd, and now sat beside me. Nervously, with tears in my eyes, I began the conversation. It was all I could do, but I had to know why His presence was still here.

"I never left," He said, "and I will always be here for them!"

Bewildered, I hesitantly said to Him, "But they don't care about You and they don't love You." There was a long pause. There was no response. All I heard was the sound of the waves crashing onto the shore.

At a greater distance, though inaudible, I could hear the voices of the excited tourists walking from one site to the next as their tour guides explained and relived the moments of biblical history that had unfolded there more than 2,000 years before. Feeling somewhat overwhelmed, I felt tears cloud my vision as I too recalled memories of my own past. I had loved someone, and her love had not been returned. I had suffered rejection by those who did not believe in me. Each time hurtful events entered my life, I grew embittered and angry. Carrying unforgiveness deep within my heart, which was filled with hatred, I had angry explosions that intimidated and brought a sense of danger to others. I had never really cared until that incredible night when I was carried into heaven and stood before God Himself. He forgave me of all of my transgressions as I forgave those who had wounded me.

After an extended time of silence, I spoke again and reminded Him that His own people, Whom He came to earth to save, had rejected, mocked, and scorned Him, and still even to this day, it remains the same. There was nothing more I could say; my emotions were getting the best of me. I sat there looking through my tears toward the water below me, not fully understanding why He was still here.

A few more minutes passed before He spoke again. When He did, His words were soft and tender. I could hear the depths of His heart and feel His emotions when He said, "I still love them with an everlasting love. I will never leave them nor will I forsake them. I will be there for them even to the end of the world!"

Such endless love, so deep, so true! This is the same love that hung Him on a cross and enabled Him to suffer excruciating pain at the hands of His merciless captors, the Romans. The violence they inflicted against His sacred body left Him marred as no man had ever been. His flesh was ripped from His back by a cat-of-nine tails as they beat Him with a furious, vehement onslaught. They mocked Him and scorned Him, forcing a crown of thorns into His precious head.

He was desecrated as they stripped Him naked and forced Him to carry a heavy wooden cross upon His weakened and ravaged body. He staggered beneath the load, going up the Via Dolorosa on to Golgotha, where they would crucify Him between two thieves. I imagined the Romans driving large spikes into His hands that had reached out to touch multitudes of hurting, poor, and dying humanity to bring forth healing, hope, and peace to all without charge.

He showed mercy and gave grace to everyone without exception. The Lamb of God's life was not taken but given as a ransom for any and all who would believe in Him, freeing them from the penalty of their sins. He died, and three days later He was alive again, holding the keys of death, hell, and the grave in His nail-scarred hands. He stripped Lucifer, the old devil, of all authority he held against the human race. Then He ascended to His Father and became the one and only High Priest, Who can, Who will, Who does continually make intercession for all mankind. He never sleeps. Twenty-four hours a day He is available to show Himself great to those who call upon His name.

My meditations were interrupted by a familiar voice coming from the tour bus parking lot. It was Gia, calling for our group to gather at our designated site. I took a deep breath, wiped the tears from my eyes, and hurried down the steps, being careful not to stumble. I had to run to catch up with my wife and daughter, who were already in line to board the bus.

As I stood in the back of the line waiting, I turned for one last glimpse at the little, old, flat-top building, wondering if He was still sitting up there. Deep in my mind, I realized I had seen inside the heart of God, where there remained a love for His people that will never be broken by time or neglect. He loves them still and they will forever be the apple of His eye.

I was still panting from the excitement of my surprise encounter with the Lord of glory! Settling down next to my wife and daughter at the rear of the bus, I didn't address them.

Instead, I chose to remain quiet, as not to reveal nor disclose my face-to-face meeting with the Redeemer, the Holy One of Israel.

Gia's voice broke through the silence and she announced our coming itinerary. Among the list of stops, one leaped out in front of the others: homemade ice cream at the base of Mt. Hebron! *Now we are talking!* My imagination began to paint pictures in my mind of Blue Bell ice cream from home as she expressed how scrumptiously delicious it tasted. Well, we'll see! Her comments made me realize she had never been to Texas where Blue Bell reigns, "numero uno."

When we arrived, most everyone exited the bus and hurried to the pools of crystal clear, cool waters at the base of Mt. Hebron. Barbara and I had more important things to do— share a big bowl of ice cream and take this opportunity to sit privately with Gia.

"There she is!" Barbara spotted her at a distance, sitting alone at a table. We casually made our way over to her with our initial greeting, "Shalom." She responded as we greeted her and asked us to sit down at her table.

Our first comments concerned the delicious ice cream and how wonderful it was. No, I didn't mention how much more I enjoyed Blue Bell from Texas; instead I wanted to discuss with her the coming Messiah.

Gia was an avid student of the sacred Torah and she understood the liturgical purposes for which it was written. I approached the sensitive subject matter concerning the coming Messiah carefully, not wanting to offend her or make myself look foolish. We initiated the discussion by asking her about her family. I saw a sensitive glow appear in her eyes, and Barbara and I felt the warmth of her love for her husband, two young daughters, and her beloved Israel, in which she had served for two years in its military.

I paused and gazed deep into her heart, which had just revealed the type of person this Jewish woman was. We shared the same deep affections for family and country and I was certain for our God. Our discussion focused on the coming Messiah, and I recognized her knowledge of the blessed Jewish scriptures as they relate to the end of the world.

My purpose was to unify what we understood will occur in these last days and Who will be the central figure Who will touch down on the Mount of Olives. This will cause a great earthquake, splitting the earth in two from east to west, forming a great valley with half of the mountain moving north and half moving south (Zech. 14:1–9).

After this, He will descend down to the wall that surrounds the old city of Jerusalem and there He will enter the east gate, the one that has been sealed, preventing concourse into this sacred city for centuries. The multitudes of remaining Jews (the remnant) will see and greet Him, falling at His feet, worshiping Him as Messiah, Lord, and the Redeeming God of Israel.

Together, we verbally lived this moment, which is sure to come. Then I asked Gia if we were in agreement concerning prophesies of the end of time. She looked at me with tears in her eyes and replied, "Yes!"

I almost screamed, "Yes, yes, yes," but I held my composure. I had to make my eternal declaration by gently proposing this scenario. I said, "Gia, through the gate on the east side, I believe the Messiah will come. Do you?" Her immediate reply was, "Yes, I do."

Then, trying to hold my emotions intact, I said, "Gia, you and I believe as one. We both are convinced through the east gate the Messiah will appear. There remains only one difference."

She said, "What's that?"

"You believe when He comes, it will be His first time; I believe it will be His second time." Then I asked her, "Do you believe you will be alive when the Messiah comes?"

Confiding in us, from her heart she said, "Definitely, yes."

Gia, Barbara, and I made a covenant that will stand the test of time! I said, "Gia, when He comes through the eastern gate, will you look to see if in His hands there are nail scars? If you see them, will you accept Him as your Lord and Savior, Messiah?"

Then there was a pause—a long, thoughtful pause. Without saying a word, Gia reached across the table, and with her left hand gripping Barbara's and her right hand grasping mine, she looked at us. With tears streaming down her face, she spoke these words, piercing the very "heart of God" as they entered the ears of the Sacred One, the Lamb of God. Her words were, "I will!"

At last we were headed for the place I had waited and longed for these last eight years, Armageddon and Megiddo, the Mount of Slaughter! "Hear, O Israel: the Lord our God, the Lord is one" (Deut. 6:4 NIV).

CHAPTER 20

ASSEMBLE THE ARMY!

The ritual was always the same with Gia; the bus had to always leave on time. I can still hear her saying, "Line up in a straight line. Identify yourself," as she popped the whip over our heads, checking and cross-checking the list of names, making sure no one was left behind. She looked at our faces, turned us sideways to see our profiles, covering everything except the study of our fingerprints. My heavens, all we were trying to do was get on the bus! She must think this country is filled with terrorists!

At last we were cleared for takeoff. Gia sat in the front seat by the aisle and I was on the next-to-the-back seat by the window. I closed my eyes and kicked back, remembering the purpose I came here for in the first place.

My mind went back some eight years before to late January, 1981. It was rodeo time in Texas. This means cowboy hats, western plaid shirts, and red-spotted handkerchiefs wrapped, hanging, or dangling from somewhere. "Big," I said, "Big" Texas western belt buckles and blue jeans. Cowboy boots were a must, made from cowhide, rattlesnake, alligator, or any skin that can be dyed and stretched. Oh, yeah, horses and more horses—palominos, paints, quarter and cutting horses, big horses, and little horses are in the competitions of bronco busting, bull-riding, calf-roping and barrel racing. Yeah, that's Texas-style rodeo in Cow Town, Ft. Worth, where everybody is welcome.

It was less than twenty-four hours before I would attend my very first rodeo. My brother-in-law, Lonnie, had purchased his four annual rodeo tickets and invited Barbara and me to be his guests. To be honest, I looked forward to it even though, by Texas standards, I was not a cowboy. I didn't wear a cowboy hat unless a Dallas Cowboy cap counted. I didn't wear boots either, but I was going anyway. The need to do something different was the reason we accepted the tickets. Fourteen days had past since my brother was murdered in cold blood. It had been a nightmare roller-coaster ride, and I was ready to take a break and get off of this ride.

I carried out the usual routine of putting our three sweetheart girls to bed. We said all the bedtime prayers, tucked them in, and gave each one the big butterfly kisses. I briskly walked down the hall, slipped quietly into bed, reached over, and kissed my wife, who was already dozing, goodnight. I had experienced a lot of insomnia lately. Again tonight, I lay there staring up into the darkness at the ceiling, with my mind going crazy. Every possible negative scenario played and replayed over and over again in my thoughts. And then it happened!

Standing toward the end and to the left side of my bed was the Alpha and Omega, Who is, and Who was, and Who is to come. I knew Him, the Almighty, the King of Kings, the Lord of Lords, and the everlasting God!

Shocked, stunned, and frightened out of my mind, I saw that the room was illuminated by His splendor. I didn't know if I was in or out of my body—dead or alive!

His first words to me were, "Alan, fear not, it is I."

Completely overcome by His presence and appearance, I was unable to move! If it had been possible, I would have fallen at His feet and cried, "Holy, holy, holy, is the Lamb!" This One, this glorious One, was the same One John saw on the island of Patmos 2,000 years ago and the only One Who can be proclaimed as the First and the Last, the living One who was dead and now is alive for ever and ever! He alone is the sovereign God Who has all power and authority to judge the world in righteousness, bring to a consummation human history, and create a new heaven and a new earth. He truly is the "first and the last." There is no other!

How could it be? Is it even possible for the Christ of Revelation to be standing here in my room in person? Why? What in the world is going on? My mind raced with questions. *Is this the end of the world and if it is not, how could I ever explain the glory of His countenance that transcends far above and beyond imagination?*

He was dressed in a long, glistening white robe of pure silk, with a sash woven with strands of gold fitted around His chest. His hair was long, rising and falling near His shoulders as if blowing in a gentle breeze. The color of His hair was translucent white, magnified by a radiant light like the sun shining in all of its brilliance from the top and the back of His head.

If the light had come from His face, it would have blinded me! His face I will never forget! It had the attributes of a lion with the familiarity of a man. Mesmerized, I looked closer at the distinctive characteristics of His face. My fascination with what I was beholding became more and more immense as I looked into His eyes. They were intense, large, and shaped like those of a lion; the color was a brilliant turquoise blue. From the outside corners, I saw small flames of fire. His lips were large and the texture of His skin was warm, rich, and ruddy. The glorious countenance of His face was, without a doubt, the Lion of Judah Who has come out of His lair to be the destroyer of nations (Jer. 4:7 NIV).

Those hands! His hands were out-stretched toward me. *Did I see the scars?* Oh, yes, I saw the scars, which signified He was not only the Lion of Judah but the true Messiah, the one and only Savior. Lying there, I was transfixed, fastened to my bed!

Then suddenly I was caught up, out of my room, and carried away into the sphere of the heavens. As I arrived, I was surrounded by multitudes of magnificent white horses, like I had never seen before. They were stunning, powerfully built animals with flowing manes and lush tails. They seemed to have an air of confidence and a presence about them. When I looked into their eyes, I could see intelligence unsurpassed by any other horse. The greatness, elegance, and beauty of the magnificent stallion would make Him unforgettable to all who might see or encounter Him.

As I ran my hand across His silky, smooth body, this immaculate animal mesmerized me. At this moment, I sensed a stirring in the atmosphere, one of intense urgency to mount this great, white stallion and ride. In a flash, we were galloping faster and faster down toward the earth. The sounds of million of horses and riders could be heard as their thundering hooves echoed from the heavens!

Strange feelings of intense emotion began to build up inside of me. It was as if my blood was boiling! We were going to war! We were undetectable, in stealth, as we continued to descend downward toward the earth. I laid my head closer to the neck of the great white horse, pressing and driving Him with all that was within me.

There were four riders in front of me. My eyes were fixed upon them as I wondered aloud who they were. The three nearest me looked like mighty warrior angels, but their identity I did not know. The nearest one was only two horse lengths ahead; the other horses were three or four lengths ahead. On my left, approximately six horse lengths in front, I saw Him riding, the mightiest Warrior of them all, the One Who is called Faithful and True.

I could see His sacred head with many crowns upon it! From His eyes, flames of fire burst forth! His robe, no longer pure white, was now stained with blood. He sat erect and upright on His powerful stallion. The more I pressed my steed to catch up, the distance did not change. I saw Him turn His head and glance at me over His right shoulder. When He did, I yelled as loudly as I could, "Who are these men?"

He spoke with a strong, loud reply, which echoed throughout the heavens, "They are warriors. Dennis is in the crowd behind you and he too is a warrior."

Though I was amazed at all that was transpiring and thrilled to hear the news my brother was accounted as a warrior and was somewhere close behind me, I never looked back for fear I might lose ground to those who were in front of me. As we descended at a great rate of speed, I saw it coming into view. It was ground zero—a mountainous valley filled with multitudes upon multitudes of armies gathered for war. Then all of us began to feel the fierceness of the anger of our mighty God, Who was leading us into battle. I was about to explode as I sensed the wrath about to be poured out by our fearless Leader.

I knew it would surpass all the world's wars combined; it would be a day of infamy that all would never forget!

Suddenly, I came to myself. I lay there trying to determine where I was. *Am I at home in Texas, or am I in Israel in the middle of the Battle of Armageddon?* As I looked around my bedroom, I shook myself and took a deep breath. It must have been a vision, and through it I was translated ahead in time.

Bewildered, I wondered what all of this meant and how I could explain this to anyone. Morning finally dawned. At the breakfast table Barbara asked, "Did you sleep well last night?"

"It was a night I will never forget," I began as I undertook the task of trying to describe the great white stallion I had ridden into the Battle of Armageddon. In the vision, I, along with multitudes of warriors and angels on white horses, descended out of heaven toward a great valley. There I saw the armies of all nations gathered together to make war on Israel.

I will never forget the look of confusion on Barbara's face. Conveniently, I left the conversation before either one of us became frustrated.

The work day brought a welcome reprieve from warring in the heavens. The rodeo would be a complete change of pace for me and Barbara. Though the two of us had lived in or near Ft. Worth all our lives, neither of us had ever attended a rodeo.

Lonnie and his wife had agreed to meet us in the great foyer of the Will Rogers Coliseum. As we entered the massive front doors and walked into the circular foyer, instantly we were surrounded by hundreds of cowboys and cowgirls, all arrayed in western clothing. As a rule, I am never intimidated by my surroundings or people. But this time, maybe just a little! After all, I was dressed in a short-sleeved casual shirt, regular blue jeans, and tennis shoes, wearing a Dallas Cowboy ball cap. I stood there, covering my nose against the offensive odors. I wondered if it was the fried onions or the smoldering hot dogs, or possibly draft beer, that saturated the air.

No, there was something more detestable than all of these combined that was causing me to gasp. What was it? Something must have crawled up and died nearby. It would not take long for me to discover what the source of this stifling odor was that was smothering me. As we walked into the second floor of the arena, there it was. It was horse manure and cow urine that filled the coliseum. I began to choke and gasp for breath. *Somebody call the medic; bring me some oxygen!* I ascertained that this foul odor must become an acquired smell and I would eventually adjust to it.

Working our way down the concrete steps near a balcony, we finally located our seats. *Wow! Way to go, Lonnie! Great seats!* This was a perfect location to view all of the events. We could see the complete arena. I stood in front of my seat with my Coke and popcorn in my hand, glancing around the massive arena. I could see thousands of people already gathered below us; at a distance I spotted my long-time acquaintances and friends, Ben and Wilma Martin. Then I heard Barbara say, "Sit down, the rodeo has begun."

Right below us and to our left was the main chute, from which the horses began charging out into the arena. There was every breed of horse imaginable: cutting horses, beautiful palominos, and my boyhood favorite, the paint horse, like the native Indians rode throughout the West. It did not take long for me to lose the initial excitement. Surely, the cowboys were having an off night! They could not stay on the bucking bulls the required time limit and the calves dragged the little bronco busters all over the place as they hung onto their necks or even tails for dear life.

What a riot! It sounded and looked as if every one of the participants and fans alike were having a wonderful time, and so were Barbara and I. And then, power failure!

Instantly, all of the lights shut down! There was nothing but darkness everywhere, pitch darkness so thick you could feel it. And then a light, a brightly beaming spotlight pierced through the darkness and illuminated the large chute below us to our left. Every eye, thousands of them, focused on who or what was about to appear. Then, for the first time ever in a Ft. Worth rodeo, appeared a horse—the horse of the ages—a white Andalusian, his rider mounted upon him without a saddle. I could tell he was a European dressed in all-black Spanish attire.

Silence filled the coliseum, as if a giant vacuum had swept across the arena, leaving the air void of oxygen and causing every man, woman, boy, and girl to become speechless! An immaculate, powerful creature had entered the arena. His very presence stunned the audience as the silence continued. Awestruck, our minds could hardly conceive or absorb the greatness of the beauty and elegance of this great white horse. It was him! Unmistakably him! The mighty white stallion who would charge into the valley of slaughter, Meggido! He was more astonishing in person than he was in my vision. This magnificent beast, with his handsome head, intelligent eyes, and powerfully built body with its silky mane and lush tail, swooned the crowd as he moved around the arena.

He wasn't trotting or running, but he was stepping as if he were marching to war. That's when I gasped for air! The atmosphere was so thick you could slice it with a sword as the presence of this mighty steed filled the arena. Then if that was not enough, as every person in the crowd was transfixed by the enormity of the moment, a strong, loud voice spoke out through the PA system and hailed the arrival of this stunning animal. He began to detail the historical lineage of this European horse, tracing his blood lines back even before Christ! And then he said it, revealing the secret of the Andalusian to these thousands of dazzled spectators—this horse was bred specifically for battle—to kill horses and riders!

That did it! I jumped to my feet and yelled with a loud voice, "From the lineage of this horse, Jesus Christ will ride into Armageddon." Lonnie jerked his head around and looked at me in shock. Barbara reached for me, took hold of my right arm, and pulled me down into the seat. She looked into my wild blue eyes and sternly said, "Calm down!"

Calm down, calm down! Who in God's world does she think she is talking to? I looked at her, my eyes wild, and said, "That's the same horse I told you about just this morning. How can I calm down?" Everyone in this coliseum saw and heard and now was a witness of the great white horse I had already seen and ridden twenty hours ago in heaven! The style, the elegance, and the beauty of this incomparable white stallion guarantee that all who ever encounter him will always remember him. He is unforgettable!

Now, eight years later, Gia's voice jolted me out of my daydreaming from the past, announcing our arrival at a mountain that overlooks the Valley of Megiddo. As we exited the bus, I pulled Gia to one side and asked her if it would be possible for me to go immediately to the top of the observation area alone, before the others arrived. She approved and assured me it would take at least twenty minutes before anyone else would be there.

With great anticipation, I hurried up the long, winding trail. My anxiety increased with each step. For eight long years I had waited for this moment! Even though, truthfully, I considered the possibility I would have arrived via a white horse, not a tour bus. I could feel my heart pounding in my chest like a drum as I walked out to the edge of the viewing deck.

I blocked out every thought, leaving only the vivid memory of my descent from heaven on the white horse, one furlong above the rim of the mountains that overlooked this storied place. *At long last, here I am and there it is! Yes, yes, yes, I have been here before!*

With mixed emotions, I was somewhat disappointed that I wasn't on the great white steed with the armies of heaven following the immaculate One, the one and only Lion of Judah. That devil, the antichrist, has yet to arrive with his rebellious demonized armies of the world. On the side of my neck, I could feel my pulse beating rapidly as my eyes scanned the perimeter of the valley, trying to determine the impossible mathematical equation of how many horses and men will spill their blood and die until the blood reaches the depth of the horse's bridle.

Staggering, too staggering for my mind to conceive! But I knew in my heart that this was ground zero for the greatest battle of all, the Battle of Armageddon, here at Megiddo, the "Mount of Slaughter." Standing there I knew one day I would return. The next time I would not be on a tour bus, but riding on a great white Andalusian stallion. *I can't wait!*

> Do you give the horse his strength
> Or clothe his neck with a flowing mane?
> Do you make him leap like a locust,
> Striking terror with his proud snorting?

> He paws fiercely, rejoicing in his strength, and
> charges into the fray.
> He laughs at fear, afraid of nothing;
> He does not shy away from the sword.
> The quiver rattles against his side, along with the
> flashing spear and lance.
> In frenzied excitement he eats up the ground;
> He cannot stand still when the trumpet sounds.
> At the blast of the trumpet he snorts, "Aha!"
> He catches the scent of battle from afar,
> The shout of commanders and the battle cry.
> —Job 39:19–25 NIV

Wait! I can't wait any longer! It has been twenty long years, some 7,300 days, since I was physically present in the nation of Israel. I have waited patiently all these years to return to Megiddo on the great white horse, even though secretly in my thoughts and meditations, I have returned more than one thousand times. Oh, have I longed for the day, "T-Day" that is, the terrible day of the Lord, to arrive.

The Bible clearly and distinctly describes this day in the book of Joel. The prophet, speaking of the end of time in explicit details, reveals the events that will take place concerning the advent of the Second Coming of Christ. My close examination of these scriptures is literally eye-opening in view of what is taking place on the earth today. Paying close scrutiny to these prophesies has made me realize that the possibility of the "rapture" of the church is near. These prophesies of Joel are not all-inclusive but are in conjunction with all the others throughout the Bible. The picture becomes undeniably clear.

All humanity presently stands at the precipice, as if we were dangling over the abyss . . . hanging by our feet. Count me as one of the billions who are trying to come to a conclusion as to what to do, wondering what in the world is going to happen next?

Meditating in the nighttime at my home, I recalled the secret meeting Christ and His disciples had on the Mount of Olives overlooking Jerusalem. He let them know the condition the world would be in as signs signal His return. "For then there will be great distress, unequaled from the beginning of the world until now—and never to be equaled again. If these days had not been cut short, no one would survive, but for the sake of the elect, those days will be shortened" (Matt. 24:21–22 NIV).

Wow! There it is—God's secret escape plan!

All of a sudden, it was as if a bright light came on in my head! My patience was almost exhausted concerning my intense desire to ride the white horse into the Battle of Armageddon. Some time ago I came to the conclusion that for me to return to Megiddo on the great white stallion, one of two eventualities would have to occur. One, I would have to suffer death; the other is that the rapture of the church would have to take place. The rapture is when the dead in Christ rise first and then the living saints of God, together with them, will be caught up and carried into heaven. In light of the revelation of the end time that Christ had revealed in the secret meeting on the Mount of Olives, I became aware that this day is soon to dawn!

Instantly, I knew what I had to do! I would call for a secret meeting in the mountains of Arkansas at a place called *Cabin Fever,* which is hidden away in the Quachita wilderness.

God knew exactly where it was; He had been there many times before!

I playfully yelled at Barbara, "Time is wasting; let's get this show on the road!" After forty-five years of marriage, she knows

I am a high-energy person, but this time I was more excited than usual, if that is possible. We headed for the beautiful Quachita Mountains of Arkansas to a secluded cabin hidden in the wilderness, overlooking a small lake in the valley below. No one was to know, not even my wife, that I had invited the King of Glory to meet me at our getaway place for a secret meeting.

At last, arrival! Unlocking the large, iron gate, I looked around to see if He had already arrived. I saw nothing! I hurried to the top of the mountain, sure He would be there waiting. He was not.

Not wasting time to even put our things away, I began my long hike down into the valleys, but I didn't find Him. I climbed up the steep, rocky mountainside, stumbling over fallen trees to where a large rolling stream flows when it rains. There was just a trickle and no sign of Him.

I had brought a chainsaw to cut my way through fallen trees, hanging limbs, and the thick, thorny underbrush. I am always on the alert for poisonous snakes—the copperhead or rattlesnake. After working endlessly and looking for Him intently for two days, I had not seen Him. I desperately needed to find Him.

Trying not to show my disappointment or let anyone know, I was becoming exhausted and discouraged at His lack of appearance, recalling that when I had talked to Him, I was confident He would come. It had been three days now and not a sign.

By noon on the fourth day, I wondered what had delayed Him. I still felt that for sure He would come. Gathering all the limbs, I picked up the thorny underbrush and dragged the big, heavy trees into a large pile and decided it was time to set it on fire because the winds had finally died. Carefully, I grabbed the gasoline container and slowly poured its contents around the perimeter of the large brush pile, then took a lighter and lit the fuel. It exploded into a roaring fire and became a burning incinerator, burning my eyebrows and eyelashes from my face and eyes.

Blinded by the heat and exhausted, I retreated backwards and stumbled into a folding chair I had placed by the edge of a small mountain lake nearby. I sat there with my face and forehead singed as I tried to gather my wits.

That's when it happened! I heard His familiar voice. At last, He had come! The joy of knowing He was here with me made me forget my face was burning. The long days during which I had labored and looked for Him were instantly forgotten. All of my disappointments were gone; they did not matter anymore. All that mattered and had meaning to me now was that He had come and He was here with me!

He spoke with compassion. "Alan, pull them out of the fire."

His voice did not startle me and I was not surprised. I had heard Him say these exact words to me twenty-one years before when I entered the arena of warfare against the kingdom of darkness and their ruler, the devil, on behalf of the captives who were possessed and oppressed by Satan. Then I had searched diligently to find and understand the meaning of His words (Jude 1:22–23 NKJV). But now I knew exactly what He was saying, to whom He was referring, and what I must do.

His voice came from over my left shoulder and close to my ear. I did not turn to look at Him. Instead, my eyes filled with tears and I remained transfixed, staring into the blazing fire. I could see them—I could see their faces! I did not personally recognize every one of them, but I knew precisely who they were! There was never a doubt I would do it.

I felt Him sit down close by. He continued the one-sided conversation about the hidden secrets He wanted to reveal, astonishing me, leaving my body paralyzed. His presence was so heavy I was unable to move.

The visitation lasted for nearly two and a half hours. The whole time I was unable to speak. I listened closely as He disclosed hidden secrets concerning time, space, and actions that will unfold as He brings the cataclysmic events to a climax, signaling an end to this present age. I can only share a portion of the secrets He revealed to me. It did not take me long to realize that this meeting was comprised of the strategies of warfare.

Then He instructed me to tell all believers everywhere to "Prepare for war; wake up the mighty men and all the warriors of war" (Joel 2:1–11 NIV). In this moment I knew that this God of heaven and earth, the Alpha and Omega, had set in place every person and arranged each event before the world was ever made.

The hidden secrets He released me to identify are that the sovereign God has placed throughout the world in strategic places thousands and tens of thousand of people He calls "Warriors." They are chosen and positioned to effectively obey His commands and achieve complete and final victory for His eternal kingdom.

He showed me faces—multitudes of faces from around the world. They are His representatives from every culture, tongue, and nationality. They are men and women, young and old. I did not know their names but I will remember their faces when I see them!

Intermingled in the vast crowd I saw professional people, laborers, politicians, sports figures, movie and television stars, commentators, and news personalities. Included among these were religious leaders from most every background on earth—rabbis, pastors, prophets, evangelists, teachers, politicians, public figures, and lest I forget, musicians, recording stars, and vocalists from throughout the earth.

He showed me the faces of people I have knowledge of. They are specifically chosen and strategically positioned for such a time as this! I will not release their names, but their general locations I can identify: men and women from Alaska, Arizona, Arkansas, California, Florida, Illinois, Missouri, New York, Ohio, Tennessee, and Texas.

One woman, a television personality, stands out from among the crowd. I saw her face with tears streaming down her cheeks. He told me of His love and admiration for her. Looking deep into her heart, He saw it filled with pain but it overflowed with love and compassion for those who are needy and deprived.

Last, a message to the Vatican: Stop the pursuit of canonizing Pope John Paul II for sainthood! Your earthly efforts are futile! His work is complete on the earth. He is surrounded by multitudes upon multitudes of saints in heaven—and he is one of these!

The visitation closed with these directives!

I walked up the side of the mountain, entered the log cabin, and made my way to the bedroom, where I lay on my bed staring at the wooden ceiling. After an extended time, I sat up on the bed and made detailed notes of His visitation. I continued to write, realizing the end of the matter was in view.

It can be seen twenty-four hours a day all over the world, emblazoned across newspaper pages, news Web sites, and on television screens, such as CNN®, FOX®, CNBC®, and others reporting the beginning of the greatest cataclysmic upheaval the world has ever known. The near collapse of the world's monetary system has brought calamity upon every nation throughout the earth. None will be spared. They corporately have hoisted their flags upside down, signaling their distress as they cry out in agony for a deliverer.

Their leaders, through desperation, have brokered rescue plans in attempts to save us from the looming disaster, but these will prove to be futile. Soon a leader will step forth out of the ruins of broken and failed promises to deceive the world. Because of tribulations that have broken down the nations of this world's resistance, they will become susceptible and submit themselves to him as their god and ruler. He will sign a covenant with Israel, guaranteeing peace and security for seven years. Soon after this, this so-called world ruler will attempt to present himself as God, performing miracles with signs and wonders and will have the whole world in his grasp (Rev. 13:3).

The peace treaty with Israel will be broken, and under his influence the armies of this world will gather together in a valley called Megiddo for one purpose! This self-proclaimed god-man's intentions are to once and for all annihilate the chosen people of God, the Jews and the nation of Israel.

In the dirt, the battle lines have already been drawn. This will be the final act of rebellion, where God Himself with His mighty army will meet and destroy evil once and for all. Then the King of kings will rule with all power and authority, with righteousness and in truth. His kingdom will last forever and ever, without end!

> I saw heaven standing open and there before me was a white horse, whose rider is called Faithful and True. With justice he judges and makes war. His eyes are like blazing fire, and on his head are many crowns. He has a name written on him that no

one knows but He himself. He is dressed in a robe dipped in blood, and his name is the Word of God. The armies of heaven were following him, riding on white horses and dressed in fine linen, white and clean. Out of his mouth comes a sharp sword with which to strike down the nations. He will rule them with an iron scepter. He treads the winepress of the fury of the wrath of God Almighty. On his robe and on his thigh he has this name written: KING OF KINGS AND LORD OF LORDS.

—Revelation 19:11–16 NIV

If you haven't enlisted in His army, do so now! God's rescue plan is simple. Call upon the glorious name of Jesus, Yeshua, the Lamb of God, confessing your sins, and He will forgive you. Stand still before Him; His awesome power will transform you into a completely different person. Walk in peace and confidence, knowing God has forgiven you, and in everything forgive those who have wounded you. Remember, at all times and through all things, look unto Jesus, the author and finisher of our faith.

Any time now, His "Escape Plan" will be implemented! See you soon on the white horse!

OPERATION TWO-EDGED SWORD

> The Word of God is living and sharper than any two-edge
> sword. It penetrates even to dividing soul and spirit,
> joint and marrow. It judges the thoughts
> and attitudes of the heart.
> —Hebrews 4:12 NIV

This book is more than just letters on a page. It is alive with God's spirit and power.

If its anointed pages have set your spirit aflame, igniting faith, hope, and a desire for the supernatural, causing you to become a minister of fire, then join with us as we kindle the flame around the globe.

1. Join us in our endeavor to care-flight this book, *Voice of Many Waters,* into the land of Israel without charge, placing it into the hands of thousands of Jews. We believe this

book will alter the outcome of eternity in the lives of God's chosen people.

2. Help us in our crusade against the enemy, who holds multitudes of wonderful people of the Latino nations hostage. With this book printed in the Spanish language, they will see and hear the voice of the Living God, Who will break their chains and set them free.

Your compassionate love and generous gifts will help us to place this book into hundreds of waiting hands in their predominate language, enabling them to hear His voice and come to know Him personally.

If your spirit has been touched by the power in this book, consider these ways to help us get the message out: Remember word of mouth is still the most effective tool.

- Give the book as a gift to someone in need
- Buy the book for Christian organizations, men's and women's ministries, church groups, prisons, and shelters
- Share with others on Facebook® and suggest that others share how this book affected their lives.
- Consider placing this book in church bookstores, or on counters for resale to customers. For more information on discounts that are available for resale and case sales (approx. 70 books) see:

www.voiceofmanywaters.com
Please designate your love gifts of support to Israel or Latino nations.
Make checks to:
Alan Youngblood Ministries, Inc.
P.O. Box 820219
Ft. Worth, Texas, 76182

We invite you to continue your experience with
Voice of Many Waters at our Web site:
www.VoiceofManyWaters.com

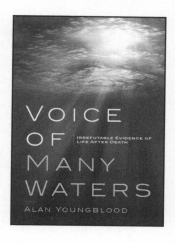

Share your supernatural experiences and discuss those of the book with others at the Forum.

Communicate with the author: alan@voiceofmanywaters.com Read Alan's Blog.

Purchase additional copies of *Voice of Many Waters*, CDs, and more.

Find out more information about Operation Two-Edge Sword on our Web site.

For information about having the author speak to your church, organization, or group, contact: alan@voiceofmanywaters.com

WinePressPublishing
Your Book, Defined.

To order additional copies of this book call:
1-877-421-READ (7323)
or please visit our Web site at
www.WinePressbooks.com

If you enjoyed this quality custom-published book,
drop by our Web site for more books and information.

www.winepressgroup.com
"Your partner in custom publishing."